Calling All Volunteers

New ideas for recruiting and managing

Dr. Jesse O. Bolinger

Copyright 2019 by Rural America Press. All Rights Reserved.

The information contained in this book is intended to be educational and is not to be used for diagnosis, prescription or treatment of any health disorder. This book is sold with the understanding that neither the author nor the publisher is engaged in rendering any legal or psychological advice. They both disclaim personal liability, directly or indirectly, for advice or information presented within. Although they have prepared this manuscript with utmost care and diligence, we assume no responsibility for errors, inaccuracies, omissions or inconsistencies.

ISBN:- 978-1-5136-5127-9
Title: Calling All Volunteers
Printed in the United States of America
For more information, including library cataloging information, visit www.jessebolinger.com.

Dedication

To my wonderful wife Chasity and our beautiful daughters Gracie and Emma: Your love and support during my education, research and writing process. It was a long endeavor, and not one that was always easily understood, but through it all you stood by me with love and support.

To my parents, Craig and Ruth Bolinger: Your love and support allowed me to gain my initial education and work experience and to understand that volunteerism is important. Without your guidance I may have never found my way to nonprofit organizations.

To Rosemarie Pelletier: Through your mentorship during my dissertation I found a topic that was more than interesting and that has expanded beyond belief in the years since our time together at Capella University.

To Jim Tussey, my early childhood and elementary school Principal: You demonstrated to me that active listening combined with compassion and problem solving can overcome objections and obstacles. But more importantly, you always made me feel that I was important and mattered. Your positive attitude about my value as a person has helped me frame how I see and value others. This book could not have happened without your contribution to how I developed as a person.

Foreword

It was another fall day at Graceland University in 2005 when I noticed a young student walking with his service dog, seemingly excited to be, or what I thought to be, a freshman at the school. Later, I saw him in the Swarm Inn (student center) reading a textbook with his face two inches from the page.

During his years as a student at Graceland, he could be seen walking to class or just being a part of the campus. Everybody knew Jesse and his dog, Kirby, and saw him studying in the library and the student lounge. He walked with a purpose in his stride and a goal to be accomplished.

When we became better acquainted, it was evident to me that his life would be dedicated to helping people. He prepared himself during his undergraduate and graduate careers to be a leader in his chosen field and a service to others. Jesse's lifelong sight condition has given him particular insight into the importance of volunteering to better reach people with special needs. During his research on how to improve the use of volunteers, he realized that little had been written about the subject. Thus, the need for a seminal treatise on the use of volunteers in today's world.

For fifteen years Jesse has immersed himself in promoting the RSVP (Retired Seniors Volunteer program) in Southern Iowa, in founding TechiePaws for training service dogs, in writing grants for volunteer service and in developing how to write grants for volunteer programs. Because of his extensive research and experience, Jesse has laid out the pathways for those who wish to volunteer or direct volunteer programs.

This book is a tribute to an exceptional man. I hope the readers will find knowledge and inspiration to assist them in developing volunteers.

-Jerry Hampton

Contents

Foreword 4
Preface 6
Acknowledgments 12
About the Author 14
About the Research 15

Section One

Chapter 1	Why are We Here?.	18
Chapter 2	An Overview of Aging.	37
Chapter 3	Generation Alpha	54

Section Two

Chapter 4	Getting Your Foot in the Door	66
Chapter 5	Leaning on Learning	75
Chapter 6	The Working World	82
Chapter 7	Crazy Happy (Mental Health)	86
Chapter 8	Have You Ever Thought About.	93
Appendix A	A Traditional Volunteer Application Form	98
Appendix B	The New Way	101
	(A newly formatted volunteer application)	
Appendix C	Interview Questions	106

Preface

At the onset of my first PhD colloquium in Dallas, Texas, my group leader Dr. William Disch asked us an interesting, and somewhat uncomfortable, question, "What is your dissertation topic?" I am positive that there was possibly only one person who had an answer. The rest of us had no idea and thought our dissertations came at the end of our journey. Dr. Disch quickly pointed out that beginning right away would allow for greater success and make it easier for us to complete our degrees and move on with our lives and careers. We were asked to return the next day with an outline of our chosen topic, with our review of the biographies of dissertation mentors, and with our choice for the top three.

In my hometown of Creston, Iowa I had been involved in the teen center, as well as working with youth volunteers as an intern at the local YMCA, so I automatically gravitated to the idea that certain factors within the lives of rural Iowa youth would impact their selection of volunteer opportunities. I found literature to support this concept, wrote the outline and returned the next day with this information. I knew my outline was not perfect, so some things would have to change. I also completed my list of three potential mentors, one of which was Dr. Lynn K. Jones. I only knew her based on her Capella mentor profile, and what came next was not expected.

The following day as we discussed our findings, Dr. Disch showed great favor for my topic, my research and even my mentors. He quickly pointed out that Dr. Jones was leading a group seated just behind us and said he would introduce the two of us later that day. Once the introduction was made, Dr. Jones asked me to connect with her again once we finished our next assignment of creating posters reflecting our topics. Their purpose was to outline our elements such as methodology, research questions, theoretical underpinning and the like.

Making hand-written posters is not one of my strong points. An advantage to being a doctor is that I now have an excuse for my poor handwriting! However, I did make my poster, located Dr. Jones and gave my presentation. While she was impressed, she was also concerned. We had been given limited information regarding the process

Calling All Volunteers

of the Institutional Review Board (the committee that reviewed research studies to insure ethical treatment of participants and proper handling of sensitive information), and she expanded on this by letting me know that any study with youth could extend the process, therefore holding up my work and my dissertation. She quickly recommending I study those around retirement age, which changed my entire plan and made everything I had done the night before irrelevant. But, because of that I found a new passion.

When writing a dissertation, a scholar is asked to come up with new research: to discover an area that is missing in academic literature, to expand on a topic, or to create a new theory. Expanding was fine, but creating a new theory would take forever. However, I greatly enjoy creating something original. I also greatly enjoy taking something that exists and molding it into something different. I knew that if I worked at it enough, I would find a topic that would benefit others and be worthwhile. The difficulty was finding a precise area to focus on. As I started to research and opened my mind to all possibilities, I discovered that retired seniors' past work experiences and education may have an impact on how they are selected as volunteers. The discovery of this relationship came by accident. If you have ever searched an academic database, you know that sometimes it takes time to plug in keywords that yield the result you want. In my case I was unsure of what my end result should be, but this turned out to be a blessing. Therefore, I decided to find connections between past education and work experiences and see how they may impact the selection of retired volunteer positions.

While I had no issues with traditional volunteer application forms that ask about interests, hobbies and community involvement because the information give insight into people's lives or how they would like to assist. I could also see them as a problem in that this line of questioning does not help the coordinators put volunteers in their areas of skill. Yes, some may have talents in gardening that they may be happy to do, but if they hold an MBA in accounting, for example, they would be more useful doing paper work. There is no guarantee that individuals will automatically gravitate to their specific area of expertise or work, especially if they are retired, or will retire soon, or are making future plans so they will not sit idle immediately after their last day on the job. Before I continue, I want to take this opportunity to encourage future retirees to leave their employment with a plan. I have talked with numerous individuals who are preparing for retirement but are unsure what to do next. Equally, I have talked with those already retired that find that they should have had a plan, and are essentially unhappy.

As I continued my research, two things happened. First, I began to recognize the value and importance of popular literature. This was problematic simply because the university guidelines required us to utilize only academic literature from the previous five years. This was not to say that we couldn't use something older, but our primary focus was to be there. Fortunately, my mentor, Dr. Rosemarie Pellettier, had the solution. She explained it was acceptable to utilize popular literature if I would lay an academic foundation with some of those references that did not necessarily have to be from the past five years, but did at least need to provide grounding so I could then state how the less scholarly literature was relevant. This was good news for me because it freed my work to be utilized in the real world versus just sitting on a library shelf or being a database record.

Second, as I worked toward the completion of my literature review, I was overwhelmed with the amount of material dealing with mental health, and, once into it, I was not able to find my way out and had no way of using it. I brought this issue up with my mentor, explaining that I was not a psychology student, was not going to be a psychologist, and therefore did not have the authority to make statements about this topic in my paper.

She pushed back, telling me that I did have authorization and could, in fact, take the definition of mental health--the biggest problem I was running into, and create my own interpretation. I could not conceive of my doing that as a student, but I quit resisting, and kept reading and writing. It was at this point that I looked at elements of the quality of a good life and, eventually, happiness. The social science definition I arrived at essentially stated that mental health is "the process or processes an individual uses to maintain who they are emotionally."

After graduation, I knew it was necessary to continue work on my research. A number of recent graduates, faculty and staff warned me that depression could set in if I did not. However, I found my direction to be somewhat unclear. I knew that, at some point, I wanted to write a book, but I felt that I would have to be much older and much more experienced before this could take place. Even though I was "an expert in my field" now that I held a PhD, something still did not quite feel right. It was not until I was attending a conference a year or two after graduation that I received the push I needed to write the text you are reading now.

I cannot recall the conference, the location or even what workshop had just concluded. What I do remember is standing in a traditionally dark hotel conference room with a man who had written a book himself. I expressed to him that I was impressed by his ability to research and write a book, and how I felt that I wanted to do this someday but did not have the skills to undertake such a project. It was at this point that it happened, the gates of reality opened and I was told to "Write the damn book!" So, I did just that, I went home, wrote an outline and, even though it has taken several years, now present to you, the "damn book"!

As I began writing, I quickly learned another lesson someone attempted to teach me in graduate school. The lesson, converting a PhD dissertation into something that the general public can read, let alone would want to read, is difficult and sometimes seemingly impossible. That comes as a result of the "academic fluff", or as a former supervisor of mine would call it, "The result of being piled higher and deeper than BS." Yet, it may have been this reality that caused me to continue and expand my research. But the expansion did not head in the direction set forth by the dissertation, it took another direction.

New York Times best-selling author Gretchen Rubin was an up-and-coming law student and even obtained a clerkship with United States Supreme Court Justice Sandra Day O'Connor. However, one day Gretchen looked around and realized there may be more to life than practicing law. As she explains in her book "The Happiness Project" she was happy, but when she felt that there was more to happiness, her journey as an author began! Her insight initiated the expansion on my thoughts surrounding mental health. The incorporation of ideas related to happiness was not possible during my dissertation research, but post-graduation this expansion was clear. The guidance provided by Gretchen through her books, podcast and live Facebook discussions have proven to be invaluable.

Acknowledgements

While the writing process is sometimes more difficult than it may appear, it is vital that every attempt is made to do so. I could not help but think about the numerous individuals who have encouraged, assisted, pushed and otherwise been a part of my education, my career and the writing of this book. If there is one lesson I have learned over the past several years, it is that I must surround myself with people who encourage and help me move forward.

First, a big thank you to my wife Chasity and daughters Gracie and Emma. They continued as they did during my dissertation process with great encouragement, emotional support and ideas. I am still amazed at the wonderful suggestions that came from children who did not necessarily understand the topic. However, I realize that even the silliest comment from a child could make my mind turn in interesting ways. As I tell my daughters from time-to-time, "When you are working on a problem, sometimes it is easier to stop thinking about it." It is that stop, coupled with funny comments, that have yielded some of my greatest ideas!

Second, I give thanks to my parents Craig and Ruth Bolinger! They have been key players in every major part of my life and decision over the past thirty-five years. The lessons I have learned from them have been life changing and have led to my attitudes about life and my desire to learn, to create and to help others. My ability to be successful with a disability comes from their perseverance during my early years as they advocated for my right to be educated in a regular classroom. This created my can-do attitude and the desire to learn as much as I could.

I also wish to give thanks to the various medical, educational and other professionals who have been a part of my development through the years. The advice, treatment and resources provided by these individuals, coupled with everyone else listed here have undoubtedly been key to my making it to this moment. First, I must thank Dr. Thomas Carlstrom. When I was just two days old, as a neurosurgeon he stepped in to give me a life-saving shunt. While I am certain that he is the one who informed my parents that I would more than likely be unable to get an education or ever lead a normal life, I also know that he recognized my successes over the thirty years I saw him as a patient.

The staff at the Green Valley Area Education Agency (now Green Hills) contributed support, guidance and friendship that was essential during my primary education. From the early access teams that met me when I was only a few months old to the individuals I still am in contact with, I thank you. I am certain that the speech therapy received from Jackie Luther has aided me even more than I realize. To Valerie Caputo, thank you for ensuring my hearing was in check and for your continued words of encouragement. Finally, to the late DeAnn Fuller, my Orientation and Mobility teacher from first grade until graduation, who equipped me with the skills and techniques to navigate independently. However, outside of these duties, she provided me with additional self-advocacy skills, friendship and, in the end, the resources to obtain my first dog guide.

Jerry Hampton is one of the greatest men and volunteers I know. While I have known him for almost fifteen years, it is only more recently that I have come to know of his strong commitment to voluntary service. As Director of the Retired Senior Volunteer Program (RSVP) at Graceland University, I saw him on a new level as I became familiar with his volunteer work and the commitment to volunteerism shared by his family. I was honored to be instrumental in presenting Jerry with the President's Lifetime Volunteer award. He has provided continued friendship and encouragement and supported my growth as a young professional.

I thank the numerous individuals who aided in editing and provided resources and general guidance. These individuals include: Dr. Tracy Connors, Dr. Geraldine Wait, Dr. William Disch, Dr. David Devonis, Dr. Constance Davis, Dr. Icek Ajzen, Dr. Cornelia Flora, Dr. Stewart McDole, Dr. Lynn K. Jones, Dr. Robert Wright and Greg Sutherland.

This book would not have been possible without the professional expertise of my editor Faye Shaw, graphic designer Ruth Seagraves and APA editor Dr. Daniel Platt. In addition, it is necessary to thank those individuals who provided feedback through readings of early versions of the book. These include my brother Jason Green, sister-in-law Laura

Green, cousin Audrey Bolinger and Jeff Jorgison.

Finally, my last words go to the dogs! Throughout my life I have been fortunate to have many pets. However, having a Leader Dog proved to be an invaluable part of gaining my independence as a legally blind individual. My first dog, Kirby, aided me in the completion of my last two years at Graceland University and through my Masters of Nonprofit Management degree. While this degree was completed online, I benefitted from Kirby's companionship that gave me the ability to work full-time during the program. Finally, thank you to my most recent Leader Dog Teddy Roosevelt. Teddy has provided companionship not only for me, but for my entire family. When at work, Teddy has proven to be even more alert than typical dog guides. The numerous trips to the Graceland University library, the public library and other various meetings have been safer and more fun as a result of his service!

About the Author

Dr. Jesse Bolinger was born with Hydrocephalus, also known as Water on the Brain, that resulted in being legally blind, therefore his future was uncertain and the odds were stacked against him. However, his two parents refused to accept limitations, so Bolinger persevered by attending the local public schools and later graduated from Graceland University with a Bachelor of Arts degree in Communications, from Regis University with a Masters' of Science in Nonprofit Organization Management, and eventually from Capella University with his PhD.

Dr. Bolinger grew up in Southern Iowa with the belief that hard work, desire, and need are the beginnings of everything great. With this in mind, he began his entrepreneurial aspirations by forming WebJOB Internet services at the age of sixteen. After graduating from Regis University in Nonprofit Management, he first formed a nonprofit organization to provide technology for the disabled, and later he created Bolinger Solutions, a provider of call center and consultation services for businesses and nonprofits. He believes that the only constraints for people with disabilities is the restrictions they place on themselves.

Dr. Bolinger has served as Director of the Retired Senior Volunteer Program (RSVP) at Graceland University as well as manager of the Annual Fundraising call center. Most recently, he has returned to the national service community as an AmeriCorps VISTA member by serving with Decatur County Development Corporation. He lives in Lamoni, Iowa with his wife Chasity, daughters Gracie and Emma, retired Leader Dog Teddy Roosevelt and a cat Lucky.

A Note About the Research

As I began work on my PhD at Capella University I had the important realization that my research would also help other people. I also wanted to write and publish as much as I could in an effort to advance our country and society.

While writing my dissertation, I had difficulty completing the literature review section. I had summarized relevant academic and popular articles pertaining to each theory or concept that I studied; however, I kept finding additional information and eventually realized that I could never read everything on the topics at hand, and that I would have time for additional research after graduation. I also understood that my own shortcomings would leave room for others to expand on my ideas.

As I completed my degree and spoke at several engagements, I received extensive encouragement to soon write a book based on my ideas and findings. After graduation, in an effort to expand on my ideas, I began reading all relevant, or seemingly relevant, material, and not just in the academic realm. The information I naturally gravitated to was centered around happiness, aging and, of course, volunteerism.

While I knew that duplicating my dissertation study was a must at some point, I also knew that a study involving generations other than Baby Boomers and older generations would be invaluable. Therefore, thanks to Graceland University, I was able to perform a second study with students, staff and faculty between the ages of eighteen and seventy-one years of age. This allowed me to explore the same themes that were in my dissertation, but to expand on the idea of maintaining one's personality through mental health. This study also allowed me to collect data on the original target generations and draw comparisons with younger generations at the same time. Results of this study brought insights that I believe would not have been found at other colleges or universities.

For those not familiar with Graceland, it is a small campus with about 900 students as of the 2018-2019 academic year. The liberal-arts university was originally founded as a two-year college by the Reorganized Church of Jesus Christ of Latter Day Saints, now the

Community of Christ. Students that attend there are typically looking for small class sizes, for the opportunity to be involved in ways that are not available at larger institutions and for the value of a liberal-arts education.

Aside from the aforementioned studies, I have found large quantities of information in popular literature. As a student I struggled with the ability to use popular literature, however, after learning how to back up popular literature with academic findings, I was able to overcome this obstacle. The ability to find connections in popular literature has given me additional guidance and motivation for this book and ideas on how to connect this text with everyday life.

Section One

During the writing of this book I learned more lessons than I can possibly count and far more than I could possibly ever teach. As I finished edits on the final chapters I realized that dividing the book into sections may be helpful to those unfamiliar with some, or all, of the material.

Section One gives a background on volunteer service, plus my experiences with the topic and information on the current living generations in our society. I am providing these insights to give all readers, volunteers and volunteer managers alike, vital information on this important topic. Generational facts are given with the intention of establishing a basis for you to begin thinking about your volunteer program or volunteer role. In these chapters, I did not necessarily make a direct connection to volunteerism, and, in some ways I did this intentionally. My goal with this book has been to bring new ideas to the nonprofit sector.

Chapter 1
Why We Are Here

"I have been volunteering for six years now since my retirement," said John. "The main reason is to be able to give back to my society. Also, I feel like I have a duty and responsibility for myself [in volunteering]...I do a lot of things...driving people to medical appointments, helping people pick up groceries...helping the visually impaired shop. Some of the jobs that I do now include photocopying, laminating, phone education with clients, putting manuals together, preparing food vouchers, Christmas exchange, school backpack program, filing, etc....

Like many volunteers, John has discovered the career skills he has learned over a lifetime are put to good use. "A lot of my skills are used in areas such as people relations, prioritizing, data input and working within time constraints." John believes these diverse challenges have kept him sharp (The Joy).

What John Duffy, a Canadian volunteer, shares about himself in "Volunteer Success Stories" emphasizes some of the points I want to discuss in this chapter.

Volunteers are a vital factor for all nonprofit organizations. Their task can be as simple as a housekeeping service or as complex as a board member assisting with strategic financial planning and development. Regardless of the function, the volunteer's background is often asked about but seldom taken into consideration when marketing for, or assigning, volunteer positions.

Considering people's past work experiences, educational backgrounds, mental health, and reasons for wanting to volunteer makes a deeper understanding possible by drawing on their specific transferable and soft skills, which in turn, leads to more rewarding volunteer positions. Successful volunteers will not only increase the quality of work completed but will additionally add to the overall standard of the organization's environment. This environment, then, will enhance programs with a potentially higher rate of goal achievement.

Participant satisfaction is necessary for a successful volunteer program. Understanding based on new research will aid institutions in sustaining volunteer programs for years to come. I ask that you keep this in mind as you consider the roles you can develop to improve the volunteer experiences in your organization and community.

The point of this chapter is to provide an overview of volunteerism for adults age fifty-five and over. It is dedicated to your gaining an understanding of why a change in the selection process is critical, what has happened in the nonprofit sector to lead us here, and what may be in the future of the selection and management of volunteers. I am also interested in reaching individuals interested in how various generations think about aging and how they can best offer their service to others. Finally, I hope to appeal to those of you who are thinking toward the future. Most of all, I am writing to the dreamers among you who are open to all new ideas that can change, not only the nonprofit sector, but our culture as a whole.

An overview of all my research will help you see the importance of the work, education, and mental health factors utilized to fill voluntary positions. This knowledge is necessary to comprehend the current concepts that will be fully outlined later. I ask that you keep an open mind in envisioning new directions for volunteer recruitment and retention. The following will help you understand my background with the topic, the events leading up to this book, and the future potential for research and implementation of volunteer management.

In 2014, I completed my PhD dissertation entitled "Education, Work and Mental Health: Impacts on Senior Volunteerism: A Qualitative Study." The title is merely a sophisticated way of saying that through personal interviews, I studied the influence of older volunteers' past experiences on their attitudes and how this contributed to their success and satisfaction as volunteers.

During the writing of this book, I learned more about the distribution of academic research and how the general public does not realize how it impacts them. For example, how many times have you read a newspaper article or watched a news program that says "according to a recent study"? The problem is that the study is never cited. Through this book I want to explain my process and show you exactly how I arrived at this information.

In my initial study, I looked at past work positions, educational background and mental health (quality of life) by using anecdotal interviews as opposed to numerical (quantitative) data. I presented a set of questions over the phone and talked with three to five participants from each of four selected rural Iowa communities: Creston, Clear Lake, Fairfield, and Atlantic with populations ranging from 7,000 to 10,000 residents. Conducting the interviews presented a few unique challenges, but also allow participants to act a little more naturally than they possibly would have in a face-to-face setting.

I made three separate calls: the informed consent, the interview, and the follow-up. The informed consent process was one of the many requirements of the Institutional Review Board (IRB) at a university or research institution which protects the human participants. Because of that, I had to read them the mandatory informed consent, and they were required to acknowledge that they understood the document.

The interview was initially expected to last about one to one and a half hours; however, many interviews were completed in half an hour to forty-five minutes. I quickly learned that many participants had an outstanding grasp of the impact their past experiences had on their retirement years. For example, one contributor hardly took a breath when asked if there was a daily activity she engaged in to keep mentally alert. She quickly responded that she worked a crossword puzzle each day, just like her mother had done.

The study consisted of ten questions, nine of which were designed as open-ended questions geared toward a given topic of the study. The tenth simply asked them to provide any additional information they felt helpful or necessary. This question existed even though the third phase of the interview process was a follow-up call about a week after the interview to collect any additional information the participants may have thought of between calls.

During that call, in many cases, I took the opportunity to thank them one last time and have a short general conversation. One person wanted me to keep her up-to-date regarding my research. In the intervening years, I have visited with her a few times and have learned that she is still volunteering and has visited with her friends about my study and this book.

A Brief History of Volunteerism in the United States

It is essential to understand voluntary service in our country, and in other countries. In my research, I have primarily utilized research and ideas from the United States, Canada, Mexico and the United Kingdom. While plenty of opportunity existed to explore ideas from countries such as China, Japan and the Middle East, the cultural differences are too great. The history of volunteering dates back hundreds if not thousands of years. It is human nature. However, formal, government-regulated organizations are a new phenomenon.

During the early to mid-1800's the idea of people helping others began to spread across the United States, in part from a growing disdain of slavery and the realization by some that anyone, of any age, could help and make a difference. In 1851, the first YMCA opened and was followed by the first YWCA in 1858. These two organizations not only played a major part in a turning point in American culture, but laid the groundwork for practices in the nonprofit and volunteer areas.

In 1881 Clara Barton, commonly referred to as "the angel of the battlefield", founded the American Red Cross. Within eight years, it moved from just providing first aid and care to soldiers to assisting during disasters like the Johnstown Flood. Today the American Red Cross develops procedures for life-saving first aid, including CPR administration, and is one of the first groups on the scene of natural disasters, house fires and other emergent catastrophes.

Near the beginning of the twentieth century, the Salvation Army appeared on the horizon. Today, many of their thrift stores contribute funding to summer camps and other programs for disadvantaged children and youth. The organization's focus is on assisting those less fortunate. While the Salvation Army is not the only nonprofit to take advantage of these stores as a funding stream, portions of our culture may use the term Salvation Army to generalize thrift store shopping. Other organizations that run similar programs came later, such as Goodwill and the Disabled American Veterans (DAV). Many of these storefronts act as training grounds and as an excellent source to engage volunteers in the local community.

About the same time, civic organizations were emerging. The Lions Club International, Junior League International, and Rotary International all hold similar beliefs and values in regards to aid and services to their local community. These often coexist and actively provide services such as cleanup, food basket programs around holiday time, and scholarships for students nearing the end of their high school career and wishing to pursue a higher education.

The first large-scale system of volunteers developed during the great depression and continued into World War II. During those times, individuals came together from all walks of life to provide food, clothing, and shelter to those suffering the most. Even the wealthiest Americans felt an impact, and a sense of urgency developed to support each other.

When the United States entered World War II on December 7, 1941, a new voluntary focus advanced as a vast majority of Americans found themselves supporting the war effort. Factories shifted their attention to the production of goods for soldiers, families rationed food and grew vegetable gardens, and volunteers provided entertainment to soldiers home on leave and to those who were recovering from injuries sustained in battle. This shift in commonality through shared purpose brought the country together and helped develop a deeper feeling that service was an indispensable part of the American culture.

In 1964 President Lyndon B. Johnson declared a "war on poverty." As a result, Americans followed their altruistic passions by serving their communities in new and unique ways. Three programs: The Retired Senior Volunteer Program, Foster Grandparents Program, and Senior Companions Program encouraged freely given service by those fifty-five years of age and older. These programs now allow individuals to serve as little as one hour per year or as much as forty hours per week, depending on an individual's interest and ability. Congress would officially authorize these programs in 1973 through the National Senior Service Act (Corporation for National and Community Service, 2018).

In 1990 President George H.W. Bush signed the National and Community Service Act which provided funding for schools to promote service learning in the classroom. The Learn and Serve America Act allowed students to learn through hands-on experiences and fostered the development of service and leadership skills. Through the remainder of the 1990's strides were continued through the creation of AmeriCorps and the Corporation for National and Community Service. In 1994, possibly one of the most significant boosts came from the designation of Martin Luther King Jr. Day as a national day of service. Each year on his birthday National Service programs perform community betterment projects and provide special presentations and programs to promote the ideal of fellowship through community service (Corporation for National and Community Service, 2018).

At the turn of the millennium, we were embracing volunteerism across the country. Then the American culture changed forever. On September 11, 2001, two planes struck Towers One and Two of the World Trade Center causing destruction, mass confusion, and chaos in lower Manhattan. After witnessing the impact, volunteers reversed the process and began supporting the families and the emergency responders who were always there to help us. At that time of crisis, President George W. Bush understood the impact of voluntary service to the nation. As a result, he called for every American to give two years, 4,000 hours, to National Service (Bush, 2002).

Since then national service has come to the forefront of our culture with resources available for individuals from all walks of life and of all ages to serve when and how they wish. Additionally, the importance of service in educational and correctional systems has become a means of mentoring while working to achieve goals. In coming years, national service will continue to expand even when faced with the potential of budget shortfalls and the desire of some lawmakers to discontinue government underwritten volunteerism.

Definitions

Through understanding the following terms as they apply here, I hope that you will have a deeper appreciation for the uniqueness of the issues related to volunteerism in rural communities across the United States.

Volunteer: An individual who donates their time and talents to a nonprofit agency. However, it should be noted that volunteers may receive reimbursement for expenses related to their service, such as meals and gas mileage.

Rural: A rural community will be defined as a community with a population between seven and ten thousand residences. Various agencies may have their own definition of the term. For example, the United States Census Bureau defines rural as "all territory outside of Census Bureau-defined urbanized areas and urban clusters."

Senior: Any individual over the age of fifty-five years of age.

Past work experience: Formal paid employment, either full or part-time.

Educational background: Formal, or informal, learning in an individual or group setting.

Mental Health: An overall satisfaction with life goals and objectives.

Urban: For our purposes, urban is defined as an area with a population of 50 thousand residents or more, as well as a high level of technologically connected and publicly available services and resources.

Traditional Volunteerism

The most traditional type is that of an individual or group being site-specific or purpose driven. Before my research began, I believed this was the only form of volunteering. As I learned, the idea of regular voluntary service is still the cornerstone of many organizations today and an important social aspect for many groups. As I will point out throughout this book, there is nothing wrong with the way voluntary service has been done in our country; however, there are ways to improve the selection and retention of volunteers. Retention may quite possibly be one of the most difficult aspects of the management process.

Traditional volunteers not only complete necessary work but also allow agencies another means of connecting with people. I have been blessed to know many individuals who volunteer in various settings. In one case, a family took cookies to a hospital once a week. While I believe that the patients there relied heavily on the physicians and nursing staff, I also know that the delivering of cookies, along with some conversation, was quite possibly just as impactful. This seemingly simple act was probably unknown to the majority of the organization, but one that had a significant effect on those involved.

It is important to mention that not all nonprofits, even those with volunteers, have formalized their process. During my AmeriCorps VISTA term, I learned that many nonprofits in Decatur County utilize volunteers, but do not impose some of the most basic things, such as tracking hours, which would be considered a vital practice by any seasoned volunteer manager.

Virtual Volunteerism

All around the world thousands of individuals have started to dedicate their time to nonprofit organizations right from their home computers. Simple activities, such as conducting web searches to more complex tasks such as video editing and database administration, are now taking place hundreds, sometimes thousands, of miles away from the home office of the organization. The new phenomenon of virtual volunteerism may directly or indirectly be attributed to the corporate shift to virtual teams and virtual work environments, but may also be attributed to a growing desire and the need to serve.

Volunteer dedication can stem from positions in nonprofits, as well as positions at the grassroots level in an unofficial capacity, to solve a problem or create a solution to a perceived problem. Support in these areas can come directly from the World Wide Web. Also, sites such as VolunteerMatch.org conduct searches to find volunteer opportunities or virtual positions in an individual's local community. The rise of virtual volunteering has also allowed those willing to give of their time to share ideas with nonprofits, which then lead to the creation of more volunteer roles and new ideas.

Volunteer hubs are springing up around the country. An Iowa example, the Volunteer Center of Iowa, aids regional volunteer centers in developing programs and assisting nonprofit agencies in recruiting volunteers. Virtual sites such as VolunteerMatch.org, along with volunteer centers, allow individuals to connect with volunteer positions in their area and online.

Although the concept of virtual volunteerism has been given little attention in the past and has not spread widely to the senior population, it has escalated and been a part of this age group for decades in a less traditional sense. Through working on projects at home such as cooking for church groups, sewing blankets, booties and hats for organizations and letter writing for political organizations, individuals have made a difference without leaving their homes.

As the application of technology expands through web-based, audio and video conferencing, the roles individuals can contribute to as a volunteer has grown. Today there is little that cannot be done virtually. The resistance by organizations to virtual volunteering comes from an overall fear of a lack of productivity or organizational oversight (Bolinger, 2010). However, one employee may perform well in a fast-paced team environment on campus while another may function better working in solitude at home on a more flexible schedule.

Informal Volunteerism

A final, and undoubtedly under-researched and underappreciated, group of volunteers are those that give informally. These do not share their time directly to an organization or an official cause but help family, friends, neighbors, and small groups that are not necessarily formally organized. While the research and examples that are the backbone of this text are based on formal ideas, it is vital to give thought to those who are quietly giving their time to people that may otherwise be forgotten or not have access to formal volunteers.

The most common informal help comes from within families and neighborhoods. In 1995 I gained quite possibly the most significant lesson along this line. I was twelve years old when I was put on the front lines of communication after a tornado ripped through the outskirts of rural Creston and destroyed the homes of two neighbors. At that time cellphones were not commonplace, so transmissions between home sites and other helpers was accomplished through a two-way radio like a citizen's band radio. These were licensed through the Federal Communications Commission, giving us more private conversations. When information needed to be relayed, I would radio someone who had a mobile unit and provide the given news or update. Many times, this would involve my being the go-between with a phone call and the mobile unit. All of this was done while taking notes and tracking any other needed information.

Through the advent of social media, informal volunteerism has expanded to the point that many do not even recognize the practice. Through sites such as YouCaring, GoFundMe, and Meal Train, individuals can learn about a need and either share this information with others in their social network, give, or do both. The application of social media for this type of support has become a near-daily practice. Within my own Facebook friends list of about six-hundred friends, hardly a day passes that I do not see an opportunity to become involved in one of these ways.

Finally, and what I consider to be possibly the most profound; providing food, companionship and other assistance to elderly family members and neighbors. This informal service is essential to the well-being of these individuals; but, as I have learned over the past few years, it can also give great satisfaction for the person offering the food or companionship. For a while, my family has been blessed to live next door to a woman who is now one-hundred years old. She was widowed in the early 1970's and has lived on her own ever since. After being diagnosed with Macular Degeneration several years ago, she has suffered a considerable decline in visual abilities and can no longer read, play the piano or cook. Yet, she still lives on her own. My family recognized her need for companionship. With my wife having a love for cooking and my children wanting to help; we greatly enjoy taking her supper on a regular basis and hearing stories from the past.

Theories

I feel it is first necessary for you to understand the theoretical underpinnings, although they are not the point of this book. Hopefully, this will not be painful, as one theory is commonly known, and the other is easily understood. I expect this will benefit you when thinking through processes for your organization or for a voluntary position and will compel you to research other ways to interpret how and why volunteers do or do not perform a certain way. First, Maslow's Hierarchy of Needs explains how individuals think and feel and what elements are vital to their success in life. Second, the Theory of Planned Behavior, portrays how an individual's past actions can be used to predict future activity.

I am not suggesting that management teams or boards review theories at meetings. However, they can be applied to existing situations and make improvements through the concepts outlined here. Although some ideas have found their way into our society, current research has yet to be employed, it is often difficult for individuals and organizations to merge theory and research-based ideas into practice. While there are some organizations that make it their mission, this is not the norm. However, organizations, such as the Dekko Foundation formed by Chester (Chet) Dekko in 1981 after his manufacturing company became successful, conduct research on youth development and then aids in the decisions of awarding grants to nonprofit organizations in communities served by Dekko facilities.

Theory of Planned Behavior (TPB)

The Theory of Planned Behavior is a widely promoted social-cognitive approach that predicts future actions and reactions based on a review of past performances (Ajzen, 1985). As I spent time researching and visiting by email with the creator of this theory, I began to realize exactly how it plays out in everyday life. While TPB is typically only applied to one-time situations, I believe it fits in areas that are recurring and pertains to volunteer behavior and management. When it is applied, the primary factor in determining volunteers' behavior is their actual intent. While it may appear odd to utilize a person's intention to measure their behavior itself, this theory has become a vital predictor of other actions (Ajzen, 1985, 1991).

The Theory of Planned Behavior identifies intention by three factors:
1) attitude, such as the volunteers' positive or negative perception while performing an activity;
2) subjective norm, or the perception that they must engage as directed by outside pressures; and

3) perceived behavioral control, or the degree to which volunteers realize they have control over their actions. It is important to point out that if people have positive feelings about what they are doing, they will feel they should engage in it. In addition, the more they recognize they have control, the more likely they are to respond in the predicted behavior (Ajzen, 1985, 1991).

When I began conducting research on senior volunteerism and looking at theories, it did not take long for me to become enamored by TPB. Quite honestly, the theory had personal meaning, as I quickly found examples both in my own and my family's lives. I compared people who had intentions and acted on them, versus those who had no plans or ambition and did nothing. It is this lack of ambition and engagement that is most concerning to me.

Why is it that some seniors can do nothing but drink coffee, watch TV, and take an occasional trip to the grocery store or doctor's office and figure that is enough and ok; while others deliberately create time to be of service to others and their communities? I feel that this intentional service is a vital part of life and longevity and is necessary to a person's well-being. It also has the potential to forge a culture shift.

In your own way, apply what is offered here and keep it in your back pocket for future consideration. My hope is that you will take bits and pieces and practice it in your own life and work.

Researchers have determined that volunteer managers should have realistic expectations of those seeking to serve. These expectations will give position seekers an increased understanding of how their skills would fit a specific situation. When they find their desired alignment, it is possible to greater predict their behavior.

It is vital to understand that intentions do not always lead to action, but they can become more forceful when combined with motivation. Gender, cultural influences and having a plan of action also impact the desire and willingness to participate. Studies reveal that typically those intending to follow through succeed more often than those who do not define their outcome. TPB can analyze self-reported behavior as well traditional data collection methods. This theory only forecasts, so consequences of behaviors are not necessarily detected or analyzed.

Volunteers can be evaluated by a variety of inventories that may be drawn from templates or developed by an organization. In the most basic forms, managers ask a series of simple questions related to their past, their beliefs regarding voluntary service, their desire to serve, and their commitment of time. These results can then be aggregated with future data collected through similar questionnaires or direct observation.

The TPB, unlike other models, is an outstanding predictor of conduct. While many psychological theories and models exist to understand behavior, very few of them can anticipate behavior based on an individual's motivations and intentions. This prediction is a vital tool for preparing for action (Ajzen, 2006).

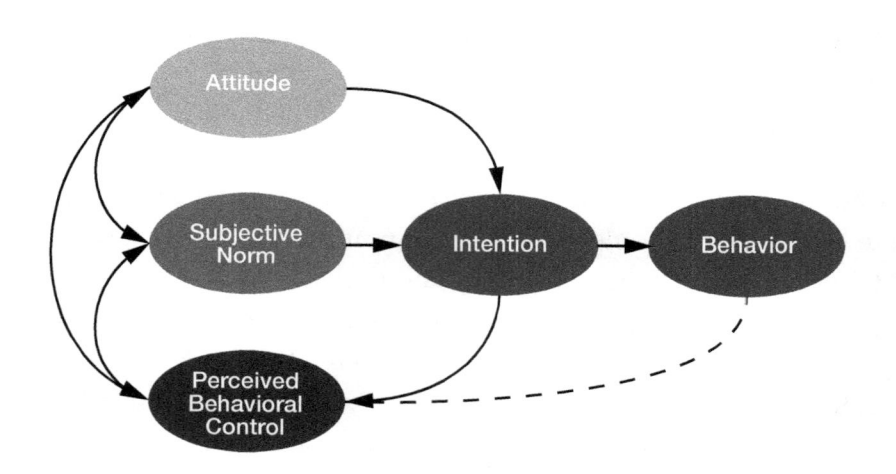

Icek Ajzen, Professor Emeritus of Psychology at the University of Massachusetts, developed the TPB model. It consists of nine elements that increase the understanding and application of the theory in our real world nonprofit setting by describing various behaviors and how they interact with one another. An analysis of each aspect of this model (listed below) will explain the how and why of behavior and factors that may influence it (1985).

Behavioral beliefs link the belief to expected outcomes. It is assumed that when performing a given behavior, people will have an expected result. For example, if volunteers engage in an activity for the first time, they may believe that they will feel a certain level of satisfaction or learn something new. However, if, they perform a similar activity as before, but in a new organization, they may believe that they will gain additional skills. Although individuals will have many behavioral beliefs, only a small portion of these will be available at any given time. It should be assumed that sharing a belief or attitude toward a behavior will strengthen the desired outcome.

Attitude entails the positive or negative value placed on any behavior. The number of beliefs that link to the results of an action determines the value of the behavior. More specifically, the strengths of each belief are weighted against the evaluation of the outcome.

Normative beliefs are peoples' perceptions of how others interpret their behavior. There are certain, preconceived ideas about how people should act and interact based on their position in life. Normative beliefs are acquired from those closest to the individual, such as family and friends. They may also include professionals such as doctors, attorneys and others with whom the individual regularly interacts. It is assumed that normative beliefs, in combination with the individual's inclination to align with them, determine the subjective norm all people expect.

Subjective Norms are expected social and cultural behaviors of engagement. Sometimes a volunteer may subconsciously choose not to act or, inversely, to engage in a behavior based on past issues related to education, work or even mental health issues. In addition, the volunteer may simply not engage as a result of a lack of interest. This lack of interest further supports a redefinition of the term mental health. It is also important to point out that subjective norms are significant in every aspect of daily life; a volunteer coordinator should be cognizant of this as it can significantly impact volunteer service.

Intention is the readiness to engage in each action and is based on all the above mentioned: perceived behavior control, subjective norms, and an attitude toward the behavior. All of these are weighted based first, on their importance to a given behavior and second, on the volunteers' morals. Therefore, elements of morality and anticipation of regret play a role in intention and decisions. Finally, regret often appears if volunteers do not like an outcome. This may also impact future engagement in an activity and personnel retention.

Behavior is the apparent response to any given situation. A single observable behavior may accumulate across multiple contexts and times so that a broader representation of actions may be created. It is assumed that the desired response is only produced when the volunteers have full control and understand their actions in the context of their behavior in their role.

Control beliefs are factors that can facilitate or impede the performance of a behavior. The assumption within the TPB model is that the combination of beliefs, along with the perceived power of each control factor, help identify the dominant control factor. Each control factor should be identifiable by how much power an individual perceives they have over it.

Perceived behavioral control is the volunteers' feeling of control in performing a behavior. It is assumed that behavior is effected by accessible factors which will differ from person to person. Specific factors, like environment, time and situation, will remain constant in all events. All volunteers will have to deal with these three areas when providing service.

Hierarchy of Needs
Maslow's hierarchy of needs

Self-actualization
desire to become the most that one can be

Esteem
respect, self-esteem, status, recognition, strength, freedom

Love and belonging
friendship, intimacy, family, sense of connection

Safety needs
personal security, employment, resources, health, property

Physiological needs
air, water, food, shelter, sleep, clothing, reproduction

Abraham Maslow was a psychologist who studied positive human qualities and the lives of exemplary people. In 1954, he created his hierarchy of human needs, a theory widely known for its views on how individuals fulfill their most basic needs, and then, progressively, their more complex ones.

I selected Maslow's Hierarchy of Needs as my second theory for this study. He outlines a model that aligns basic human needs in the form of a pyramid, with lower order needs placed at the bottom and higher, more complex needs placed near the top. Let's look at how this impacts volunteers. Starting at the bottom:

Physical needs are the most basic for human survival. These include food, clothing, and shelter. We may assume these are in place for our volunteers. But, if needed, acquiring information on a volunteer's basic needs can be difficult and is a topic that should be approached with tact and compassion. This should only take place when information or situations are presented that make you aware that a negative situation may exist that is harmful or may cause great hardship for the individual in question. Discussions about such conditions should be done in private, and nothing should be forced on the individual. Asking someone what they need versus telling them what you think they need is the best way to assist in resolving these circumstances.

Safety speaks to our natural need for predictability in our world. It is essential to have reliable outcomes, processes and protocol in place to provide a safe and stable environment for volunteers. They should also be prepared for what could go wrong: how they are expected to react in handling a questionable situation, how to report what happened, and how to confirm that they are ok. This may mean calling the police, or locking the front door at night.

Love and belonging is a higher need on Maslow's pyramid, and can make the climb more difficult. They make the climb increasingly difficult as a result of each individual's understanding of the concepts of love and belonging and their attitudes toward each. The concept of love and belonging is experienced differently for every volunteer. Are they giving or receiving love and belonging or both? It is this need that, in part, triggered the changes to Maslow's concepts that I will explore shortly.

Esteem deals directly with how we view ourselves. While a strong self-concept aids in personal advancement and success, it is not necessary for basic survival. Esteem needs are met through optimism, goal setting, and positive self-talk. It is problematic to assume that people are volunteering because they have time, money, and background experience and that equates to their having strong self-esteem. That belief can cost you volunteers. It is meaningful to have processes and training for volunteers that build self-reflection and self-evaluation, and to combine those with positive, supportive feedback on the contribution a volunteer is making to your organization. All this can give them an overall sense of esteem and success.

Self-actualization is the realization of an individual's full potential and talents. It means for people to accomplish everything they desire to do, and can do, in their lives. These people have a high awareness of themselves and the world around them. Maslow considered self-actualized people to be quite rare. This concept is not necessarily achievable by everyone. Part of this is because some individuals do not know how to attain this level, and others do not have the knowledge and resources to do so, even if they were familiar with the concept.

Within his hierarchy, Maslow believes that each lower-order need must be satisfied in sequence before the next one can be fulfilled. Although basic human needs are met in much the same way, they are achieved differently by each person. An understanding of which level volunteers are functioning provides insight into what they may be able to offer by way of service. The act of benefitting others may help them feel more actualized (Maslow, 1943).

Meeting Volunteer Needs

Each of us is unique, and even members of the same family have distinctive behaviors although they probably hold similar values and beliefs. Therefore, it is logical that each of us will approach meeting our fundamental and higher-order needs, as proposed by Maslow (1969), in diverse ways. It is equally reasonable that the resources available to people will vary, or at least be accessed differently. Meeting basic, lower-order needs is often done in much the same way by all individuals. I would suggest, however, that this has changed because of technology and other societal shifts.

Maslow proposed five areas of basic human needs. More recent research performed at Arizona State University, shows that the pyramid can be modified to recognize the importance of family and relationships. The adjusted pyramid establishes the following changes (Kenrick, et. al., 2010).

ASU's hierarchy of needs

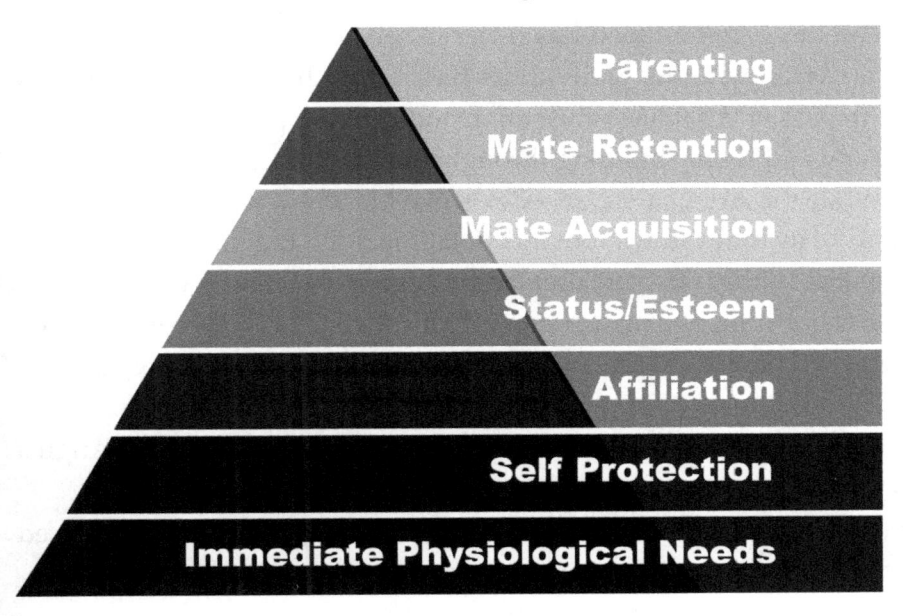

- Parenting
- Mate Retention
- Mate Acquisition
- Status/Esteem
- Affiliation
- Self Protection
- Immediate Physiological Needs

Immediate psychological needs are substantially the same as in Maslow's original proposition.

Self-protection is on the same level as the concept of safety on the original pyramid. The difference in the new model is that it places increased importance on the concept of self.

Affiliation recognizes the need for individuals to be involved with others. This concept allows them to build and maintain relationships of all sorts, ranging from family and friends to coworkers.

Status/esteem highlights the importance of social status and interpersonal feelings created by acceptance and acknowledgment by others.

Mate acquisition is vital in the new model. This element emphasizes the importance of having a romantic partner. While some individuals will resist this concept, research shows that those in committed relationships are happier and lead healthier lives.

Mate retention introduces to the pyramid the idea that humans should remain faithful to each other. While divorce rates in the United States have increased through generations and the percentage of divorces for second and third marriages is higher than first marriages, it is vital to make every attempt to stay in the same relationship. This will help eliminate stress and allow for increased happiness and productivity by both partners.

Parenting/Parenthood has replaced self-actualization on the Arizona State pyramid. Individuals have found having children allows them to pass on vital life information and increase personal happiness, longevity and legacy building through fostering the next generation.

While the Arizona State model is like Maslow's Hierarchy, it does expand to include family, romantic relationships, and parenthood. The divergence within this version places a higher level and robust focus on the acquisition of a mate, retaining this mate and finally moving to the role of a parent. These additions are helpful life experiences that mature individuals bring with them into a volunteer experience.

Other adaptations of this concept have also been issued. In August 2017 I discovered an exciting variation of the pyramid. Instead of self-actualization at the top, this version, by an unknown author, placed the concepts of morality, spontaneity, creativity, problem-solving, and acceptance of facts at the top of the structure.

After comparing these versions, my feeling is that an expanded pyramid, based on Maslow's Hierarchy, better accommodates a wide array of life experiences that potential volunteers can then reflect on and leverage for future goal setting and expectation setting.

Is only one pyramid right for everyone? Does employing existing models make sense when interviewing, selecting, training and evaluating volunteers? I believe that yet another adjustment is needed and propose a pyramid that incorporates education, work, and mental health.

While I realize that we have yet to focus on these areas individually, I want to suggest now, so you can consider how to develop, support and retain your volunteers by identifying these three key areas separately and incorporate them into a structured belief system. If you are a volunteer, I ask that you visualize what your individual pyramid

Bolinger's hierarchy of needs

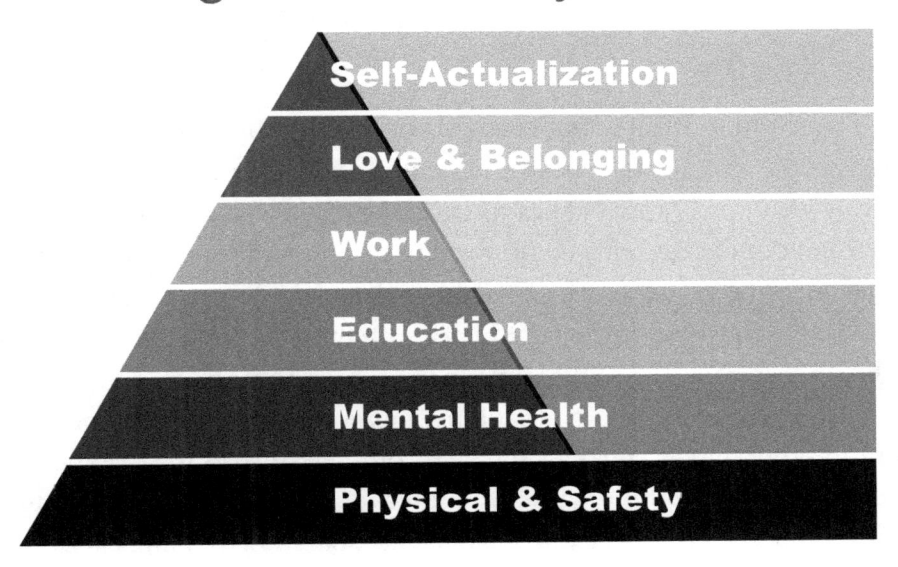

- Self-Actualization
- Love & Belonging
- Work
- Education
- Mental Health
- Physical & Safety

may look like, or what pyramid may best fit your needs. For many, the most difficult of these additions to understand will be the concept of work. If you are like many individuals, I am guessing you see your work as earning money. However, as I will propose later, there is more to a job than the money, more than socialization and more than doing tasks for others.

In this model, I understand that I have removed some levels. However, in doing that, I did not necessarily take away the need for a given task. It is my belief that through education, work and mental health, individuals will achieve other key life elements.

The pyramid structure I am introducing allows for increased applicability in everyday life. It also has better-defined categories to evaluate or improve the lives of volunteers and those who work with them.

With the foundation of volunteerism laid, history and a theoretical groundwork introduced, it is time to begin breaking down these concepts and finding applicability. We now have a basis for reflection on specific elements and for planning for future activities and actions.

Chapter 2
An Overview of Aging

As a child in rural Iowa, I never lacked opportunities to visit with older people and, quite honestly, I got along with them better than those of my own age. I cannot count the number of conversations I struck up with older Crestonians while waiting for my mother to check out at Easters' grocery store. The two red chairs parked near the entrance were training ground for me, and I am sure those experiences were part of the underpinning of my interest in the senior population.

I learned at a young age that longevity ran in my family. One Great Grandmother lived to be over 100 years old. Because of the distance, I did not get to spend time with her. However, I was able to participate in her hundredth birthday party where she shared her feelings and insights about spanning two centuries. Her children, my mother and the cousins of her generation filled in blanks on the history and events that occurred during her lifetime.

I was more fortunate to frequently visit with my mother's maternal Grandmother who lived to be the age of ninety-six. During those casual visits two things always took place: first, she showed great pride in each of us for our respective talents, and second, she told stories. I know with absolute certainty that these two things were what got me interested in genealogy.

However, I am also certain that her memoirs are partly responsible for my great respect for other generations. As I pointed out in the introduction, there are times that I am questioned regarding my interest in post-work life, including senior volunteerism, and why I live my life the way I do base on my actual age. It is my regard for the past and those insights that have given me my vicarious perspective of retirement life and senior volunteerism. These elements are what predicated my interest and desire to learn about and help others.

The Relevance of Generational Traits

The breakdown into generations may differ from person to person, but typically, people think of specific years that define any given generation. For example, Baby Boomers are those born between 1946-1964 because the post-war period saw a dramatic increase in births. Because of differing viewpoints, it is more important to determine a generation by shared beliefs and ideals.

Presently, there are six classifications in the American culture:
The Greatest Generation (GI Generation) 1901-1926
Mature/Silents 1927-1945
Baby Boomers 1946-1964
Generation X 1965-1980
Generation Y 1981-2000
Generation Z 2001-2011
Generation Alpha born after 2011

As a volunteer, exploring these groups will assist you in discerning the various shifts in our culture, in volunteerism, and in organizations. Additionally, it will aid you in reflecting on your own generation and how your personal values align with theirs.

For volunteer managers, a review of each group's values will allow you to gain, or strengthen, your understanding of the ideas commonly held among each. While deeper awareness of the characteristics may not impact the overall management of your volunteer program, it will help in constructing role descriptions, in training, and in selecting the best practices that more likely cannot succeed without recognizing what is important to your volunteers and where values of each of you intersect and differ between generations.

The Greatest Generation / The GI Generation

The Greatest Generation is most often defined as individuals born between 1901 and 1926, and those over age ninety-two are gone now. This group was mostly raised by parents who served in, or were impacted by, World War I. They lived during a time of change and turmoil in the United States. Members of the Greatest Generation include a large subgroup of those who served in the military through two world wars and foreign conflicts that occurred during this time span. They themselves would serve in World War II or support efforts at home to secure a victory and what they hoped was a lasting peace. A second element of the development of this generation was the great depression. As a result, individuals of the Greatest Generation learned the importance of teamwork and the impact it would have the on war, the depression recovery, and the progress of the nation.

A strong moral character was highly valued by this generation. They were community-minded and had a near-absolute standard of right and wrong. With this standard of morality, marriage was a life-long commitment and birth outside of wedlock was unacceptable.

Their widely held belief system also expected duty to country and service to community groups, schools and other associations. Therefore, highly organized and prescriptive organizations were created or supported by them. This included benevolent, patriotic, faith-based, political and conservation-based groups. These after work and weekend activities allowed for a balance so that even when "off the clock," a person was still contributing.

The ability to build and work in teams drove people of this era to develop lofty expectations for work and production outcomes. The GI generation did not believe in "retirement". Instead, they endorsed succession based on merit, production, and loyalty. They worked until they could not work any longer. This generation gave birth to the labor unions, which sometimes controversial, have changed the face of the American workplace.

Because of social and economic factors, this generation developed views on what they needed, or did not need, in daily life. A common phrase was "use it up, fix it up, make it do, or do without." While other generations may have similar values, none have such a deeply held value of how items should be used, or how people should make do with what they have. This GI group believed that items should be paid for with cash and that credit should be avoided. While this generation may not necessarily have had a large amount of savings and wealth, they were more likely than younger generations to have a lower amount of debt later in life.

Technology during their lifetime has seen the greatest advancements. Many of this generation saw tremendous advances in electricity, television, radio and transportation. A frame of reference is that these individuals would have been preschool age when the first flight by the Wright Brothers occurred.

Famous Members of the GI Generation
Entertainer and humanitarian Bob Hope
Entertainer and comedian Red Skelton
Newsman Walter Cronkite
Actress and singer Judy Garland
Entertainer Betty White

The Mature/Silent Generation

The Mature, or Silent Generation, is most commonly defined as individuals born between 1927 and 1945. This generation grew up during the great depression and later, a time of expected conformity in the United States. However, they also experienced the post-war euphoria and expansion that took place after the end of World War II. Abundant jobs, a changing agricultural scene due to mechanization, growing suburbs, the birth of television, an abundance of cars, rock 'n' roll music and even the Playboy Magazine made life during the Silents' formative years fun and memorable.

Like the generation before them, the Mature/Silent generation experienced war. They saw the United States become involved in both the Korean and Vietnam wars. Exposure to these conflicts created opposing opinions and social alignments within groups of like-thinking Silents. Members of this generation volunteered to assist in, or oppose, the war effort. This becomes more evident during the start and expansion of the Vietnam conflict.

Many of these were the first in their families to graduate not only from high school but from college. As they became employed, they did more than "go to work". They had careers that contributed to the rise of large corporations and the creation of the corporate culture. This culture shift would see employees committed to working for the same company for their entire careers. They were the first generation that earned their retirement.

The Mature/Silent generation is seen as the wealthiest, freely spending group. Members of this generation have also become known as the generation that, at least within their own confines, feel that retirement means that they live their final days in traveling, comfort and peace. However, as the tail-end members of this generation aged, several shifts were taking place. In smaller communities, it is not uncommon to find individuals who are still working, returning to work or volunteering where they have a personal connection. Members of this generation are noted for helping their communities in unique ways.

As young people, acquiring an education was important, and knowing and comprehending what was going on in the world was paramount. As a result, members of this generation tended to be avid readers and believed strongly in the traditional newspaper and the press. This belief later translated into connecting to their community by getting involved in activities that are close to home and supported by younger generations.

Famous members of the Mature/Silent Generation
Actress Marilyn Monroe
Boxer Muhammad Ali
Entertainer
Johnny Carson
Singer Elvis Presley
Politician Madeleine Albright

The Baby Boomers

The Baby Boomer generation, or Boomers, is often categorized as being individuals born only in the 1950s. However, they are more typically defined as being born between 1946-1964. Unlike other generations, the Baby Boomers are often split into two groups. The first holds a strong "save the world" mentality and strong beliefs on how they should be involved in effecting positive change. The second, the "Yuppies", came later and lived their formative years in the 1970s and 1980s.

Early Baby Bombers understand that there was a potential for real social change outside of wartime and focused on political involvement while members of the later Boomer generation often felt too busy with their own lives and jobs to be involved in their communities or community organizations.

Unlike members of the Mature/Silent generation, Baby Boomers look upon retirement as an opportunity to live life in new ways after their children leave home. Members of the Boomer generation were the first to be creative with new hobbies, embrace lifelong learning and travel with a purpose. They see retirement allowing them to truly do things they want to do instead of sitting in a rocking chair.

The ability for Boomers to volunteer expands as they age. Utilizing technology, they recognize that it will only continue to advance. As a result, they adapt their understanding of how the world changes and their desires to be politically active, to find ways to impact their local communities. Baby Boomers are quite possibly the first to begin their voluntary service before they retire and carry it over into their retirement years. This is often done with organizations that have impacted their lives or those of individuals close to them.

Famous Members of the Baby Boom Generation
Singer and songwriter Gregg Allman
Actor, producer and director Ron Howard
Politician and former British Prime Minister Toni Blair
Performer and songwriter David Bowie
Singer and activist Arlo Guthrie

Generation X

In some ways, Generation X, 1965-1980, may be one of the best known and most discussed generations. This could be a direct result of the changes that took place in our culture regarding technology, social change, and economic factors. With these new developments, they became more involved than the generations that preceded them.

While previous generations have demonstrated the ability to "pull themselves up by their bootstraps" and to create their own paths, this can be mostly found in the lives of our immigrants. However, with the combination of parents supporting greater access to learning and almost inherent technology skills, members of Generation X experienced a burst of entrepreneurship and creativity.

Members of this generation have not received a great deal of recognition, or even discussion, regarding their voluntary service. In his 2000 US News & World Report article, David Marcus points out that this group is often recognized more for their bad behavior than the good they do for society; for example Erik Rudolph, who hid out in the Appalachian Mountains after being accused of planting a bomb at the 1996 Olympic Games in Atlanta. Nonetheless, a much more positive, and under-recognized side of this generation exists (Marcus, 2000).

In 1993 the AmeriCorps program was created by the Corporation for National and Community Service. This approach allows members to serve in their own community while working or going to school. Unlike AmeriCorps VISTA, AmeriCorps members provide direct service to their community. After just four years, AmeriCorps enrolled their 100,000th member. It is unfortunate that such work by well-meaning Gen Xers has gone virtually unrecognized. While members of other generations have participated in programs such as AmeriCorps, AmeriCorps VISTA, Peace Corps and other programs, the idea of service by these individuals has been overshadowed by negative and seemingly reckless behavior that the news media, and perhaps our culture, finds more interesting.

While working on this book, I conducted a formal study utilizing three groups at Graceland University. One participant, I'll call Mike, indicated that technically he is a member of Generation X, but he feels more like a Millennial because he has lived most of his life during that period. In part his feelings about his own generation versus the one he identifies with come from the fact that he has spent most of his life assisting others and learning more about how he can be a better servant to his community.

While other generations may have individuals that feel the same as Mike, our culture saw such a political and societal shift at the end of the 1970s and beginning of 1980s that this is not surprising. While we have experienced similar shifts in the 1950s and 1960s, the reality for members of Generation X appears to be much stronger and took root during their formative years.

Famous members of Generation X:
Actor Robert Downey Jr.
Rapper Dr. Dre
Singer Janet Jackson
Football standout Brett Favre
Singer Mariah Carey

Generation Y (Millennials)

The most talked about generation to date was born between 1981 to 2000. Is the buzz that cause this a bad thing? Not really. This generation has plans to capitalize on their experiences to advance themselves and the human race. The Millennial generation has a strong desire to help others at the cost of personal sacrifice. As the first generation to truly grow up with technology, they have become forward thinking and have expanded what is possible. Additionally, they understand the importance, and the downfalls, of constant contact with others.

Millennials had increased "street smarts" and the ability to care for themselves from an early age. Latch-key kids of the 1980s, while having increased independence, also grew up with greater social isolation which stemmed from the time spent home alone after school waiting for single parents, or parents driven more by their careers. This generation experienced an increased number of divorces.

As a Millennial myself, I must quickly point out my profound association with technology was much higher as a child because of my visual impairment, but, as I have grown older, I find that other members of my generation are just as tied to technology as I have been.

Additionally, the cultural and societal beliefs of Millennials place a strong focus on service to others. They better comprehend why problems exist and what solutions are possible. Millennials are constantly connecting and looking for new ways to overcome existing problems and prepare, in advance, for new issues and societal shifts that will take place in the future.

In his 2002 State of the Union address then-President George W. Bush called on every American to give at a minimum 4,000 hours, or two years, of service to the nation through participating in a national service program such as AmeriCorps, AmeriCorps VISTA, and other programs (Bush, 2002). While this type of service had not been forgotten, the impact of September 11, 2001 changed the way many Americans viewed the nation and the needs of members of their own community. Millennials, in particular, found it necessary to give of their time and talents. As they completed high school and pursued college degrees the need to serve became even more evident to many.

Now, as an older Millennial, I sometimes feel like an outsider when I converse with younger members of my own generation. This may, in part, be a product of my upbringing and spending a great deal of time with many individuals who were much older than me. However, associating with my younger generation peers has given me a fresh look at the world and confirmed my own ideas about positive change for my community and our nation.

In Aug 2017 I was in Philadelphia for AmeriCorps VISTA Pre-Service Orientation (PSO) along with about 190 individuals who were preparing for action in VISTA. While the training focused on the ins and outs of service time, it was also an opportunity for us to learn about the ideas and solutions of others.

After I exited the shuttle bus, entered the hotel, and began meeting my fellow VISTA members, I felt out of place. I wondered if a year of service was a good idea for me because I felt too old to be starting this process. However, as I began to listen to others, and they asked me to share my own experiences and ideas, I realized that a year of service would truly be one of the greatest things that would ever happen to me.

During the writing of this book I have truly learned the value that members of the Millennial generation place on what they have to offer. I met a young man no more than twenty-two years' old who told me that he had spent most of his life going in and out of foster care or being homeless. He had lived in over twenty states. When he became aware of the AmeriCorps VISTA program, he knew that in service to others he would also be helping himself because he would be able to use the small stipend to improve his life. Beyond that, he could tap into his past experiences to identify the populations he would best be able to benefit. In the evenings, he even spent time in the local homeless community after our sessions ended. He used this as an opportunity to gain additional perspectives on poverty issues.

As we have seen through the discussion of previous generations, it has been uncommon for them to identify with service during their younger years. Millennials, however, have quickly sensed that is not only vital to their community and the nation, but vital to their own development and, in many ways, necessary for their personal happiness. This insight will most certainly continue as members of this generation age. Through conversations with several of them, I have been told again and again that being of assistance is necessary, and something that they always looking forward to doing.

During one interview a young woman told me that as soon as she moved to college, one of the first things she did was go to the local nursing home to visit with the residents and see how she could be of service. She had also done this on an informal basis in her hometown. She indicated that helping others is important to her and the education and work she has undertaken are a direct result of her desire to help others. When I asked her about her future plans and what she sees herself doing in retirement, she quickly stated that she would volunteer, and more than likely work with older people, because that is something she greatly enjoys.

Famous members of Generation Y
Actor Ashton Kutcher
Prince William
Singer Justin Timberlake
Singer Taylor Swift
Singer Carrie Underwood

Generation Z

In the summer of 2017, while standing in line to get on the Tornado roller coaster at Adventureland Park in Altoona, Iowa, for once I was not thinking about this book. However, I could not help overhearing two young ladies. One was talking about her job and school, but then she started talking about her utility and cellphone bills, plus other expenses. Then, something amazing happened, she started talking about saving for retirement. Listening to this conversation made me realize the importance of money and security to members of Generation Z. Members of this generation born between 2001 and 2011 understand the impact of a financial recession and have strong political views. Many also have parents who are already talking about retirement or are retiring. Generation Z is also cognizant of social issues and the need for change.

While many may think that this generation is simply plugged into technology for communicating with their friends and engrossed in social platforms, it extends much further into educational, work, and general mental engagements. Members of this generation have come to understand how relevant it is to live a healthy life and know that physical and mental health is something to be valued.

Generation Z is the first to grow up with the ability to volunteer virtually. However, many still choose to engage with others through more traditional or even typically informal methods. The casual approaches are viewed as volunteer endeavors because they are providing something that would otherwise be lacking. In many cases, they care for their own family members, for neighbors, or friends of people they care for in nursing homes that are not otherwise served by traditional programs.

Generation Zs are demonstrating that they understand community needs and manifest a desire to help others. While some of them may appear to be zoned out and uninterested, this lack of regard may simply be an absence of proper engagement by those wishing to gain attention and actionf. To motivate them, it is vital to provide them with messages and information that demonstrate how they can serve in a given situation, and how their support can provide a positive impact.

The way Generation Z will engage in their retirement years is yet to be established. However, they have certainly grasped the necessity of helping others and are sure to follow in the footsteps of previous generations through national service. As I have looked around my small Iowa community over the past four or five years, it is not difficult to find the work being done by young people. Even our mayor recognized the necessity of input from young people. As a result, the Mayor's Youth Council advises him on a variety of youth-centered issues. Young people also engage in National Service programs, local community, and civic organizations. It is my firm belief that this will continue throughout their lives and into their retirement years.

Famous members of Generation Z
Media personality, reality star and model Kylie Jenner
Model Presley Gerber
Model Sofia Richie
Actress Lily-Rose Depp
Model Taylor Hill

What Happens in Retirement

For generations there have been a number of age biases. I am sure you have heard that forty is "over the hill," but, more recently, that fifty is the new forty. However, I am certain that you have also heard that when someone retires, they are going to turn into a couch potato and do nothing. In 1992, country legend George Jones made reference to the fact that older people do not have to conform to a given lifestyle. In "I Don't Need Your Rockin' Chair" Jones points out that "retirement don't fit in my plan." In the years since the release of this song, millions of Americans have changed their beliefs about retirement by taking some time off before changing careers or exploring new interests.

Today retirement has become a stage of life that many Americans look forward to to explore a new interest, or an activity that, for whatever reason, had been postponed. Growing up I remember asking various people what they did for a living. I recall many of them, after giving me an answer, followed it up with the comment that "I still don't know what I want to be when I grow up". At the time, I took it as a joke, but I know now that a certain number of these folks honestly meant that they wanted to explore other career options after retirement.

While growing up, my dad told me time and time again that I needed to go to chiropractic school. I toured Palmer College of Chiropractic but did not feel like I could handle the science side of things. Now I know I could have. Years after graduation, I visited Palmer again. It was on this trek that I learned of a seventy-five-year-old man who was about to graduate. It was always something he had wanted to do, so he decided to be a chiropractor in his retirement.

While picking up a new skill or taking on a second or third career may work for some, it may not be a good idea for others. As I demonstrated in Chapter Two, members of older generations have pre-defined ideas about retirement and may choose to live life out as they observed from previous generations. Gaining useful skills, taking on different careers or learning new things may not be satisfying for everyone. The way an individual chooses to live out their retirement years will depend on their own personal values, how their friends choose to live out theirs, and thoughts and feelings of family members. With this said, it is important for me to point out that the clear life direction someone has at the beginning of retirement may not turn out to be as accurate as they believed it would be.

Perceptions of Aging

I must point out that our collective perception regarding aging may quite possibly come from the way popular media portrays older people. Films like Grumpy Old Men (1993) characterize older people as grumpy who lack facing the reality of their aging, while the 1981 classic On Golden Pond demonstrates just the opposite. This film depicts the positive aspects of aging, including optimistic life changes that can occur and the happiness that can be found.

We need to be aware of our perpetuating the perception that older people are not willing to adopt new mindsets. This may seem obvious, but to come to this conclusion has taken me several years. As I have researched, it has become painfully obvious older adults are not used to the speed in which our culture is now changing. Consequently, one of the biggest impressions that exists is that older generations are not able to keep up with technology and the popular culture, and that those volunteers simply cannot do certain things. In many cases, this may be the result of our cultural myths.

In 1969, Robert Neil Butler, physician, gerontologist, psychiatrist, author, and the first Director of the National Institute on Aging, coined the term "ageism" to describe discrimination and stereotypes experienced by older individuals. Over the past several decades, the amount of prejudice, in both the workplace and every-day society, has increased. While laws have been enacted to attempt to stop discrimination based on age, it is not uncommon for an employer to simply pass someone over and state that other reasons exist for the individual not being promoted or even hired for a given position.

While there have been attempts, through state and federal laws, to address ageism as a negative element of our culture, the enactment of such laws, in many ways, has aided in cementing in stone the idea that ageism is an anticipated occurrence.

Is this judgment molding your potential volunteers to act in the way they think they should behave, or can you, through your efforts, coax out into the open the potential volunteer holds within them? Can you train them to celebrate hope, vitality, playfulness, imagination, ingenuity, and passionate behavior?

In the past our culture has assigned specific ages with certain work or job-related tasks, such as mandatory retirement for airline pilots at age sixty-five (Jorgenson, 2017). Research and our current culture are showing that this may not be the best practice. Despite this shift, ageism continues to expand through the idea that there may be a certain age where individuals should stop doing things. I will use driving as an example. Poor health, lack of sleep, illness or cognitive decline may cause someone to become an unsafe driver. Does age alone make a person a driving hazard? Does it alone make someone a less potential volunteer candidate?

I am going to be clear that, in the context of this book, the term "senior volunteer" is not a by-product of ageism. The term is a classification with a starting age and no ending upper age limit. We can predict outcomes and the pros and cons of being involved with our volunteers, but we can't predicate outcomes on the age of the people.

Ageism is not simply found in older individuals. Reverse ageism, essentially thinking that younger people act or believe in certain ways, is also found within our society. Ignoring age when considering reverse ageism in terms of volunteer management can aid in assigning roles based on education, work experience and mental health.

In some ways, I may have even discriminated against myself when I was considering writing this book. As I mentioned in the introduction, I thought I had to have twenty or thirty years under my belt in my field before attempting it. However, being the product of an excellent doctoral program and having a number of quality professional experiences prepared me for this research and writing process. It aligned me with the people necessary to make this text possible at a time when it is truly needed, and not when I felt that I was personally ready.

Forced retirement, or mandatory retirement at a certain age, is not found as frequently in the workplace today as it once was. However, this is primarily the product of federal legislation, and voluntary retirement is still found in many organizations. Giving an individual the choice of termination or taking voluntary early retirement with full retirement benefits can still be a form of ageism.

Elements of ageism exist in social settings as well as the workplace. They may be less obvious as there are no legal elements that protect individuals. They can be found in comments such as "that person drives like an old grandpa" or "those pants look like something my grandma would wear." Avoiding ageism in everyday situations can be difficult, as many generations have picked up on this through popular media and other social cues.

What does this all mean?

When thinking about how to capture my thoughts and share them, I did not anticipate talking about anything other than individuals over age fifty-five who volunteer. Yet, as I reviewed my own work and that of others, I realized that a discussion of generations needed to take place. Exploring the interplay between generations helped me gain clarity and focus on how limited my approach had been towards a valuable volunteer base. Just being open-minded didn't cut it. An understanding of different generations, their values, and beliefs, as well as how they view voluntary service, is vital. In this chapter I wanted to share with you the factors to examine in selecting voluntary positions.

By considering our current cultural beliefs, we give nonprofit organizations, volunteer managers, and our society in general an opportunity to begin making positive changes to advance the nonprofit sector. That will make it possible to provide better recruiting and training to individuals who want to be of service, and who may otherwise be missed or overlooked.

Over the next several chapters ponder your own generation, your personal values, and your understanding of the perceived values of your generation. Together we will explore ways to move past the perception, expand the dialogue, and look at ways to tap into your volunteers' potential.

Calling All Volunteers

Chapter 3
Generation Alpha

Social researcher, author, and thought leader Mark McCrindle suggests that a new generation has emerged. He poses that generations may not change every twenty or thirty years, but instead, are now defined by characteristics and behaviors. As Generation Alpha advances, certain skills sets and behaviors are magnified or newly existent ones appear. Members of Generation Alpha are those individuals born between 2011 and 2025.

When I began working on this book, the idea of Generation Alpha had not even been announced. Quite frankly, I had realized I could define it, but I just could not come up with a name for it. I knew however the generation was defined, it would have increased technology skills, but my uncertainty was in how this generation would interact socially. As my research continued I noticed other indirectly related elements of generational studies. For example, Apple Computer developed a new coding language, Swift, and Swift Playgrounds which allows even young children to learn to code and become developers. At Apple's 2016 World Wide Developers Conference, it was announced that Anvitha Vijay, the youngest developer to ever attend the conference, was just nine years old (Apple, Inc., 2016)! It was this revelation that made me realize that younger and younger children would not only learn to code and utilize technology; they would discover and create, not only for themselves but, for the masses.

Generation Alpha will be the most technologically advanced and literate generation to date. While some scientists believe that the extensive time this generation is spending with electronics is negative, others believe that it will be well spent come adulthood. A year ago a long-time friend told me, speaking specifically of his four-year-old daughter, "One of my five is in that span. She quickly picks up anything to do with technology and learns it on her own. Hand her a phone or a tablet, and she knows what she is doing." When asked if he could give me a specific example he stated, "She can play games, swipe to see pictures, and run the Roku to watch both Netflix and Hulu." While this example illustrates a child using it for entertainment value, it demonstrates that, at an early age, children are gaining a basic understanding that when a command is given to an electronic device, something happens.

On the same day, as the above example, I also received a message from a relative regarding her children born between 1997 and 2011. Reflecting on how her children grew, she saw little difference between the child born in 2007 and the most recent born in 2011. In part, she attributed this to her, and her husband's decision to not introduce them to technology early. While it is arguably possible to keep technology away from children, it has become increasingly difficult in today's society.

As technology expands, changes come to our education system and attitudes regarding the workplace shift, so it is easy to imagine that Generation Alpha's world will be much different than that of prior generations. It is important to remember that they will face challenges that we have not even conceived and will have educational and career opportunities that have not yet been developed. At one point during the writing of this section, I had the opportunity to speak with staff members at the Iowa STEM Initiative and at a foundation that funds youth programs in several states regarding career exploration and education children should receive regarding potential careers. While one expressed that we should be thinking to the future and talking to children about ways to consider careers and technology that does not yet exist, the other explained this type of thinking was not possible, and it was more important to place the focus on developing strong young people who have the ability to engage with society and utilize current technology.

It is understandable that technology is vital to the advancement of our society. However, as I visited with parents of young children and reflected on my own childhood and my children, I realized how important socialization is, and it will remain so. Members of Generation Alpha are predicted to be less social as they grow. Some researchers and studies suggest this is a direct result of their increased interaction with technology. While this concern is understandable, it is important to consider the ground that has been covered by previous generations.

As a millennial, I can paint a clear picture of my experience with technology. My path was much different than that of my peers.

Growing up on a small family farm in rural Southern Iowa one would think that I would have been one of the last kids to access technology. However, over the years I have come to realize that access and utilizing technology at an early age may have been one of my greatest advantages to overcoming a visual disability. I learned to apply basic computer functions, word processing, and even the basics of HTML and web design while many of my friends were just learning how to type and play games. This advanced learning allowed me to consider other aspects of technology, including networking, e-mail, messaging and discussion boards.

Between 1996-1998, the idea of instant messaging became popularized. This made it possible for individuals to connect any time they are online and allowed for socialization at school to carry over to home in the evenings and on weekends. While we most certainly spend a great deal of time talking on the phone, we discovered it was much faster to IM a friend or group of friends. Instant messaging was so popular, that I have to personally admit to constant use. So constant was my use, that I was known to instant message a college friend who lived right across the hall from me. We did this with both of our doors open. Yes, we could have talked back and forth, however, we found instant messaging more efficient because we could send a message, continue work on our studies and respond when we had time.

As I graduated high school and started college, I quickly noticed that many of my friends began to access something called The Facebook, it has obviously now been shorted to Facebook, and even two and three-year-olds know what it is and how to use it. As this and other social media platforms have developed, the way we communicate is changing once again. While this impacts adults, as instant messaging did, it is mostly affecting those growing up with the technology. Instead of texting, young people now simply send a Facebook message written in text shorthand or through a series of emoticons, or icons that represent words. For example, they may say "C U L8r" instead of "See you later." Or, through emoticons they could say, "I am on the 🚌 head to the 🏫 ." In this example, the individual means that they are on the bus headed to school.

It is believed that members of this generation will be lonelier and quite possibly more socially isolated. While they are just now beginning to turn six and seven years old, it is still possible for these behaviors to begin. The potential for isolation may be attributed to technology; however, it is also vital to remember that technology can also connect individuals.

With prior generations, primarily Generation Y and Z, concern has been expressed regarding the amount of time children spend watching television, playing video games or working on a computer. With even earlier generations, primarily Baby Boomers, it was felt that sitting too close to television could hurt their brains, and that being too close to a microwave could harm their eyes. However, as we have discovered, neither of these beliefs is true. Therefore, it is not surprising that new studies and research is showing that certain types of gameplay can actually be helpful to brain and social development.

It is not surprising, especially with the expansion of technology, that members of Generation Alpha are becoming more aware of world events and social issues. What may be surprising, however, is that members of this newly defined generation are so concerned that some parents find it difficult to get their children to refocus from a given issue. Increasingly, they are becoming more and more involved in social issues and finding the ability to speak out on issues they find important.

While technically a member of Generation Z, it is quite possible that figures such as Kid President have revolutionized the idea that children have a voice and can be a part of social change. The influence of Kid President quickly filtered to members of Generation Alpha, his messages have encouraged young children to convince their parents to aid them in working on social issues that members of this generation value. One of the most recent examples of the intense need to help others can be found in four-year-old Austin Perine. After learning that people can be homeless, he told his parents that he wanted all of his allowance to go to chicken sandwiches for the homeless, once a week he feeds as many homeless people as he can and always tells that "don't forget to show love" (Hartman, 2018).

As a result of this awareness, it is not difficult to make predictions about how generation Alpha will respond to volunteerism, and about how it will be much different from today's landscape. The volunteers will certainly be engaged in social issues and those dealing with human rights. Children of this generation are often-times responsive to news stories that deal with people suffering and animals in need or distress.

While I pointed out earlier that children are learning technology on their own and through their parents, there are also those who are being kept away from it at all costs. What does this have to do with volunteerism? It has everything to do with it! When the idea of Generation Alpha and its self-isolation came to my attention, my original prediction was that this would be the people that, as working adults and retirees, would volunteer virtually. However, based on comments from parents who withhold technology from their young children, this could change.

As this chapter began to take shape, I found myself having conversations with residents of Decatur county regarding poverty. As I worked with no systematic approach in terms of generations, I began to see a pattern. Members of the GI and Mature/Silent generation started to talk about their childhood and the values they learned and how that has impacted their later life. Though these conversations, I came to realize that in many ways, a drift back to these values would be helpful for our society.

Concerning volunteerism, this would mean that members of Generation Alpha would not be self-isolating, rather, they would be helpful and available to their neighbors. However, this would be coupled with their immense understanding of technology. The way generation Alpha chooses will depend on how previous generations have cared for the planet and the advances that will be made with technology and societal issues. While this can be said for today's retirees, this will be magnified by the time generation Alpha begins to retire in 2066.

The education Generation Alpha receives will be much different from that of previous generations. While members of Generation Y were the first to experience online learning through fully online and hybrid classes, members of Generation Alpha are finding it possible to attend virtual school, beginning with kindergarten. For student success, attendance and traditional discipline will still be necessary, along with parental participation.

Education

Members of Generation Alpha are focusing on mathematics and science in new ways. With the growing STEM (Science, Technology, Engineering, and Math) emphasis in the United States, students as young as second grade are beginning to learn multiplication and division and, in some cases, even algebra. This type of early education is helping these students gain an early interest and understanding of computer programming, web design, and other technologies. Companies such as Apple Computer are encouraging early learning through school field trips to The Apple Store and workshops designed specifically for children to learn skills such as graphic design, video editing, and programming.

As I began high school in 1999, I found myself in classes and meetings that presented "Iowa 2020." The discussion typically centered around what the state would look like, and the student skills and industries that would need to exist. At the time, I thought talk about the increased focus on math and science was ridiculous, and I equally thought that changes in classrooms and learning styles was crazy! Surprisingly, many of these discussions did not miss the mark by much, so I now realize that conceptualizing what will happen in education for Generation Alpha will not be that far off either.

In many ways, we are already beginning to see shifts in teaching styles and classroom design. I recall walking into a classroom with my own girls and being shown different seating options for them and being told that these options are available so each student can have a different experience. Besides, many classrooms I have now seen have implemented specifically designed areas for students to work and study based on personal choice. For example, one classroom had areas designed for reading or writing. If students do not want to sit at their desk, they can move to where they can either sit, lay down or lean against something.

As technology advances, so too will virtual schools. Although they are still relatively new, many states have already embraced the idea by approving companies, such as K-12 and Connections Academy, to operate in the state. These virtual public schools function much the same as traditional schools, having a similar structure and utilizing the same learning materials. This approach is appealing to many families because it offers flexible school days for families that travel or have other commitments that have to be met during a traditional school day.

Virtual schools have not yet taken on the form described when I was younger. Then, when the topic of virtual school would come up, the term "virtual school" was not even used. I would hear something like "someday kids will learn from a robot standing at the front of the classroom," or "there will be a robot that will teach kids at home." I am not saying that we will not get to this point; however, I find it difficult to believe that traditional teachers, virtual or not, are going away soon. At least in the case of K-12 online and for my children, Iowa Virtual Academy which is run by the Clayton Ridge Community School District through a partnership with K-12 Online, has a structure that allows for flexibility in a student's day, time with a state certified teacher and interaction with peers though field trips held across the state.

Finally, higher education will change as well. With the advent, not only of fully online and hybrid classes, but fully online colleges and universities, students are finding themselves faced with the need to be online to interface with even the most basic face-to-face college or university course. However, mobile technology has made this increasingly simplistic. The days of remaining in a residence hall room or library to study and submit assignments may be over, as now it is possible to submit an assignment while walking to a friend's house or sitting in the local coffee shop. It is difficult to say what the landscape of higher education will look like in ten to eleven years. What is certain is that the way students interface with classes and socialize will but much different than today.

Work

Recent research makes a strong case for career education beginning as early as the fourth grade (Adams, 2016). Starting this soon will hopefully encourage students to place a new focus on school attendance and to find new ways to apply learning earlier in life. For students at the lower end of the economic ladder, this type of early education may prove helpful in finding a way out of poverty. For students at the middle and upper end, this type of education may prove to foster longer and more successful careers.

The way they will experience work will also surely change. With a growing demand for work-at-home positions, an increasing number of companies embracing this style of work, and an ever-changing technology, the number of individuals that telecommute is sure to increase exponentially. Also, the number of totally virtual organizations may also expand. The most important thing to remember about Generation Alpha is that they will be the generation to grow up in a fully digital world. The way this generation learns about work today will influence their type of learning and the way they interface with technology and society.

Attitudes toward working will be important in an ever-changing global environment. With the expansion of the internet and mobile technology, the ability and necessity to connect globally are sure to expand. As I read and talk to people who work virtually, one of the things I consistently hear is that they can make their own schedules and work from just about any location they choose. While it is unlikely that our society will ever get to a point that individuals have total control of their schedule and work location with absolutely no restrictions, it is likely that the idea of a well-balanced work life is one that will be highly sought after by this generation.

As an already socially conscious generation, Generation Alpha can be predicted to expect their work to be meaningful. I would think that will take on a number of forms. First, meaningful work will make a difference. While we will still need accountants, bankers, cooks, doctors and other types of service professionals, the need for human and public services will also increase. Today, it seems that just about every time I log onto Facebook, there is an article about jobs that will no longer exist. While there is some truth to this, what these articles are missing is, that while a specific job may not exist in ten or twenty years, a job that disappears does so because something new has happened. So, just because the traditional job of pilot may not exist in twenty years, it does not mean that the job of an airplane controller will not.

Calling All Volunteers

Mental Health

One of the biggest points that stands out for me concerning Generation Alpha is that they are predicted to be self-isolating. In my mind, as hard as I try for it not to be, this is a negative--not because it is wrong, but because, in many ways, our society has social and cultural norms that portray isolated individuals as having something wrong with them. While there are examples that support this, it is not necessarily true of everyone. The isolation being experienced by members of Generation Alpha occurs because of their exposure to technology, and/or because of their family activities, and of parents who do not want to expose their children to the every-day stress and negativity currently taking place.

As a student at Creston High School I had a history teacher, Randy Hughes for those of you who attended CHS, who frequently said that "history repeats itself." At the time, and possibly until about ten years ago, I thought this statement was quite possibly crazy. After the birth of my oldest daughter, I began to rethink it. As she grew older and began to ask questions about how the world worked, I began to use this phrase myself as a way of explaining how something worked or to let her know that if something happened once, it would most likely occur again at some point in the future. My research in education, work and mental health trends within the various generations, led me to realize that history is repeating itself with the current generations, and most certainly will do so with Generation Alpha.

The elements of history that will repeat are those that will make people happy and those that will bring people together. While this may seem contradictory, it is important to remember that something can repeat in different ways. As I pondered, and observed happiness in this generation, I have concluded that what makes them happy are simple things, and when they have conversations they are deep and meaningful. Repeating of history will be how they deal with hard times and the fact that they will be isolated, yet connected, with a large network of people.

The things that make children happy today are much the same as the things that did when my parents and grandparents were growing

Calling All Volunteers

up. Things such as simple play and learning new things. However, the difference with this generation is they are gaining happiness by not only in understanding of a topic, but also in having an awareness that they can be involved and make an impact.

As this generation grows older, they will have different peer pressures than prior groups as primarily the result of technology. As a result of this increased pressure, it will be necessary to develop new, and possibly more frequent, ways of maintaining their mental health. In an age where modern medicine has proliferated with medications for just about everything that can be wrong with a person, it will be easy for them to quickly and easily find that all they have to do is take a pill to feel better instead of using their own brainpower and self-identification to maintain who they are.

In short, the same strategies that are being used by retirees today to maintain mental health, such as doing crossword puzzles, reading a book or going for a walk, are the same that Generation Alpha can utilize, starting at an early age. Developing these habits and attitudes toward life early will help today's youth to not be so self-isolated that we end up with a society filled with increased mental illness and unhappiness.

Final Thoughts

One of the most difficult lessons I learned while earning my PhD was that once completed, I would be an expert with a license to think freely and be able to use research to make predictions and conceptualize. This chapter has truly given me the ability to do just that. In its original form, this book did not contain a section on Generation Alpha. However, it was a conversation with fellow Cappella University graduate Dr. Jack Bishop that turned that little section into a chapter of its own.

The views expressed in this chapter are truly my own. While some of what I state is based on some research, a great deal of what you have just read is from my own personal experiences, conversations, and thoughts over the past fifteen to twenty years. As you close the book on this chapter and after you have finished the book in its entirety, please remember that Generation Alpha is our future, what we do today will impact them tomorrow. Our world can change for the better, or for the worse. In either case, Generation Alpha will be the decision makers!

Famous members of Generation Alpha
TV star Ocean Maturo
YouTube star Lightcore Chas
Instagram star Ben Hampton
Musical.ly star Tilly Mills
YouTube star Russell Franke

Section Two

Section Two is designed to give you insights into the three key areas of a volunteer's past that I truly believe should be explored. These will properly assist in placing volunteers and aid them in selecting appropriate positions. In this section we will not only explore the impact of past education, work experience and mental health, but we will also understand how the searching and screening processes can be adapted. I will ask you to allow your memories and imagination to run wild. As with the chapters in Section One, I will not connect everything to volunteerism. Please be reflective as you read and consider the future of your organization or role.

Chapter 4
Getting Your Foot in the Door

Searching for volunteer positions or for nonprofit volunteers can sometimes feel like a daunting task. However, I have concluded that, in many cases, this is made more complicated than necessary for both parties. One reason is because they both are often looking for a perfect match and only consider placements that meet all of their expectations. When looking at volunteers' past, two things take place: first, they both gain a deeper understanding of their skills and true ability; and second, they sense the possibilities of new volunteer roles. Those tasks, based on the background of the applicants, can aid nonprofits in thinking outside the box and finding solutions that may otherwise be missed or discounted.

Many organizations, and many volunteers for that matter, often consider only the most obvious needs and only those with specific job descriptions. Also, they both sometimes disregard the value of the volunteers' services, for they are not viewed as skilled experts. Instead, they should be looked upon as just that, competent individuals that can do a professional job.

Rather than going through a long and tedious process to hire a specialist, managers need to recognize that volunteers are professionals, and that professionals volunteer. That realization can save nonprofits a great deal of time and money while still achieving the same goals.

The Nonprofit That Needed a New Building

In October 2017 I attended the Iowa Nonprofit Summit and heard a true story about an establishment that needed to construct a new building. This procedure can be long and expensive. Hiring an architect alone can take several months and several thousand dollars in design time and resources. This is what happened.

The nonprofit organization needed to build a new structure and was trying to decide how to go about it. Somehow the word got out to a local architect who volunteered to do the entire design process completely free of charge. However, because the company did not see the high quality of this offer, they turned the volunteer down and went through the extensive process of considering their requirements, seeking bids, and asking architectural firms to submit drawings of their proposed ideas. Finally, they decided on a design. When they interviewed the architect who created the chosen design, he commented: "I offered to do this for free and was turned down, now you are going to pay me to do the exact same work."

Recruiting

The difference between recruiting volunteers versus recruiting employees is that volunteers are not necessarily going to relocate to fill positions unless, of course, they are serving as part of a National Service program like AmeriCorps, AmeriCorps VISTA, other national programs, or serving during a major disaster. Therefore, recruitment efforts must be specifically targeted to the type of people you wish to have as volunteers. This can be done through local media, websites, social media and partnerships.

An absolute must for all volunteer recruitment in small communities is:
    A website for the organization
    Social media profiles (Facebook, Twitter, etc.)
    Facebook exchange and swap groups
    Local newspaper support
    Local businesses that encourage volunteerism

As part of the search, consideration should be given to partnerships with National Service programs such as AmeriCorps, AmeriCorps VISTA, Foster Grandparents and others. This does not replace paid staff, in fact, this is a violation of Corporation for National and Community Service Guidelines, but it is a great source of volunteers and resources (Corporation for National and Community Service, n.d.).

When thinking about partnering with these programs, it is important to remember that each has specific requirements concerning what volunteers may, or may not, be able to do and what may be required of them and the volunteer sites. Maintaining connections with these programs can be helpful and should be specifically considered for special events.

Applying

All nonprofits and potential volunteers should expect a formalized process for applying to volunteer. As I have pointed out in proceeding chapters, the way volunteers job search, and the way nonprofits search for volunteers should change to focus on past experiences and elements that make and keep volunteers happy. The standard volunteer application should be adjusted to include education, work experience, and mental health. Making this change is not difficult. I have included a sample adapted application at the back of this book.

The problem with this shift is that both volunteer managers and volunteers need to begin to think differently about the recruiting, training, and retaining of volunteers. Doing this will forever change the face of voluntary service and, over time, will create longer-lasting volunteers who will engage in specific roles that make them happier. As younger generations offer more service, they too will be able to connect with their past and mental health in each aspect of their assistance.

While the application form is a necessary part of positioning volunteers, understanding them and the organizations on a more personal level is essential for a successful, long-term match. For this reason, it is vital that both parties spend time discussing three key elements: the organization, the person and the position. During this discussion, the volunteers can learn more about the real inner workings of the post and organization, and the volunteer manager can truly learn about the volunteer.

While a discussion should typically follow the application and selection process, my vision of this is more a casual conversation instead of a "job interview". Obviously, it is important to have some structure to the process, as it is important for both parties to have some questions in mind going into the interview. However, I believe it is important that both parties ask questions during the evaluation. I envisioned an interview that could include one person asking a question, then the other answering and adding a query, and so on. Through this process, both parties will learn more about one another, and about the position.

Both traditional face-to-face and virtual connections can be the same! It is equally important in the virtual environment that they both maintain a good working relationship and visit frequently. While, in a traditional environment, these two parties will interact more frequently simply because they will see each other, virtual volunteers also need frequent, possibly daily, contact and have the same opportunity to discuss and learn about the organization and position. Communication should be in a way that feels natural. With virtual interviews, especially those done by phone, it is sometimes easy to interrupt one another; therefore, it is good to have small, 3 to 5-second pauses follow the end of a sentence or thought. This gives the other party the signal that they can begin speaking.

Questions asked may include:
From the volunteer manager
Why are you interested in volunteering here?
How often are you available?
Have you volunteered with our organization before?
If so when?
What similar volunteer experiences do you have?
What have you learned from previous volunteer positions?
What related experiences have you had?

A great deal of this information can be found by reviewing the submitted application; however, asking these questions will insure that the volunteer manager is getting the most up-to-date information from the applicant.

From the volunteer
Why do people enjoy volunteering here?
Are volunteers able to pick up additional responsibilities if they are successful in their original position?
Do you recognize volunteers? How?

How are volunteers scheduled?
What do you believe makes a successful volunteer?
How are volunteers given feedback?
Do all the volunteers ever get together to share experiences, ideas, etc.?

Training

Volunteer training can take many forms. However, it is important that all of it includes a few basic elements:

An introduction to the organization
A background of the organization
An introduction of staff members
An overview of programs
An overview of basic policies and procedures
A tour of the facility
A list of expectations from the volunteer

The volunteer orientation process should be designed so it can be held in a group setting, but also easily adapted to train one or two volunteers when required.

As I have indicated previously, the training process should be conversational, even if they are in a group. For virtual volunteers, every element should be included, including a tour of the organization. The virtual tour for volunteers, and other stakeholders for that matter, is a great way to help everyone feel welcome and connected!

Through the expansion of technology and the newfound utilization of virtual volunteers, it is important that all training is designed to be interactive. With screen sharing and connectivity services such as Google Hangouts, it is now possible for individuals to connect as if they were in the same room. However, virtual training does not mean that any above elements should be eliminated. Volunteers should still be introduced to all staff members, even if they will not be interacting with them. They should be made welcome in the office at any time, so local virtual volunteers, or those from halfway around the world, should feel free to stop in and say hello.

Retention

Retaining volunteers is possibly one of the most difficult parts, other than recruiting. Keeping them is a matter of motivating and understanding what drives them. Equally important is the volunteers' challenge to understand what motivates their managers. While this may seem illogical or unnecessary, that ability of the volunteers will aid in a better, longer lasting relationship.

Inspiring volunteers is something that can be easily overlooked by some organizations. At times, the assumption is made that they are motivated and will stay because they enjoy what they are doing. While this can be true, volunteering is like a regular job, and they may tire of what they are doing, especially if they do not believe that what they are doing has value, or that they are not appreciated. It is vital that volunteers are told thank you every day. This simple expression can greatly boost their feeling that what they are doing is recognized and that they are making a difference.

It is important to remember that some people are motivated intrinsically (naturally), while others extrinsically (from outside influences). Being aware of this at the beginning of their service is essential to successful volunteeer retention. A great method of giving them incentives is the Five Appreciation Languages concept, originally developed as the Five Love Languages by Dr. Gary Chapman, and adapted for employees and volunteers by Chapman & White (2012). Through this approach, it will be possible for the manager and volunteers to better understand how they, and others, are motivated. Performances are more likely to increase when people are recognized through proper rewards.

The five languages:
- Words of affirmation: Use positive words to communicate messages.
- Quality time: Dedicate uninterrupted time to listen to ideas, thoughts or stories.
- Acts of service: Provide assistance, "What can I do to help?"
- Physical touch: Shake hands, high five, etc.
- Tangible gifts: Give gifts, most often food.

Determining an individual's language can be accomplished with the Five Appreciation Languages quiz at http://www.5lovelanguages.com/profile/appreciation/.

A simple application of this language is not enough. It is necessary to offer rewards based on the above list. This will require collaboration between the administration, the staff, board members, volunteers, and other stakeholders.

Various reasons for people wanting employment can be found through even the most basic survey methods. Those who work at non-profit organizations do not necessarily work entirely for pay. Instead, they work for non-monetary rewards. Even so, managers should find small inexpensive, ways of saying "thank you" to staff members (Royal College of Nursing, 2008).

In my 2009 Master's thesis I pointed out ways to show appreciation to employees which can be applied to volunteers too. These ideas, originally published by Kelly Services, Inc. (2009) demonstrate the intrinsic and extrinsic factors that motivate employees. They also demonstrate how to show appreciation for volunteers, in this case, without spending a great deal, if any, money (Bolinger, 2009).

1. Learn what your employees want from coming to work. The most common reasons for working are money, recognition, satisfaction, and promotions. However, these elements can vary from organization to organization based on cultural background.
2. Give positive and constructive feedback. The process of motivating others is not a one-time task, but continues forever and it can, and may need to, change over time. Honest feedback, good and bad as long as it is constructive, assists volunteers in continuing to do their jobs well, and also helps struggling individuals perform better.
3. Give praise in public and criticism in private. This rule would show that managers really care about people and not just products and services. It is sometimes easier to express negative

than occasional positive feedback, but a shift in this direction can cause a change for the better.
4. Recognize that there is no "I" in team. This can make the team feel good and keep the collective motivation intact. All employees, regardless of position, want to know that they are contributing to the overall success of the department and organization. It is always nice to give recognition to individuals for a job well done, but the same should be done for teams on a regular basis.
5. Give respect to all employees. This is a great motivational tool that costs the organization nothing. Every employee, either conscious or subconsciously, wants to know that they are respected and valued.
6. Empower the staff by simply giving all employees the opportunity to contribute to the decision-making process and to help solve what they see as important problems. Accepting their input can potentially give them a feeling of ownership of their position and a feeling that their time and talents are going to better the organization.
7. A formal recognition program, either an annual or a once a month event like an employee-of-the-month can mean a lot. Rewards can range from recognition in public areas, such as a spot on a wall in the lobby or on the organization's website, gifts of some kind (such as gift certificates), tickets to sporting events, special parking spaces, and plaques are low-cost options that can encourage individuals to enhance their performance and feel they are working for a purpose.

Separate (If you have to, I guess)

The Man's Prayer, found on the popular Public Television program, The Red Green Show states "I'm a man, I can change, if I have to, I guess." As strange as it may be, this is the first thing that popped into my mind as I began considering the process of volunteer termination while I was working on a volunteer training manual for the Decatur County Development Corporation. I was also working on this chapter at the same time. The conclusion I arrived at is this: letting someone go is not something everyone has to do; however, if it is something that has to be done, "I'll terminate you if I have to, I guess."

Releasing a volunteer may be one of the last things a manager may think they will ever have to do, and for those that have done it, it can be uncomfortable. It often comes with a stigma because many do not feel it should ever happen. However, as with traditional employee situations, it may be required.

The process of volunteer termination should be conducted much the same as that of an employee. It should follow up after a warning. When the final conversation arrives, the volunteer should be asked to meet with the coordinator and a supervisor or a member of the Board of Directors. This will reduce the likelihood that the volunteer feels singled out by one person. The discussion should begin by thanking the individual for his or her service and a discussion surrounding the issues leading to the discharge. Finally, it should be made clear that the individual's service is being ended.

Unlike employee termination, it may be a good idea to share with volunteers why their services are no longer needed. By providing the reason, or reasons, and having a discussion with them, it may be possible to provide positive feedback, allowing them to create a positive change and be successful in future volunteer positions. The goal of termination is not to belittle the volunteers, but to remove them from an unsuccessful situation.

Chapter 5

Lean on Learning

Learning is quite possibly the cornerstone of our lives, whether we recognize it or not. Formal education allows us to gain a basic understanding and applications for our reading, writing, mathematics and other subjects.

Knowledge is delivered in a variety of ways: face-to-face, online, teleconferencing through webinars, formally and informally. While many may think of being educated as sitting in a classroom looking at a blackboard, marker board or computer screen, it is important to realize that volunteers have their own unique and preferred modes of learning, as well as a preference for retaining and applying the information.

The idea that education impacts seniors when selecting volunteer positions came to my attention as I began to explore why and how they choose certain positions at nonprofit agencies. Before working with them, I believed that those desiring to volunteer simply went to an organization, filled out an application form and were matched based on their interests. As my exploration continued, I learned that, while it was possible for them to utilize their interests in selecting a position, a more effective method may be to consider their educational background.

For individuals fifty-five and older, acquiring a higher education may have been difficult, depending on their age. Those who are just now fifty-five to sixty-five, no doubt, at a minimum received a high school diploma, and many also went on to college. For people sixty-five and older, attendance at college would have been possible; however; this would have depended on their upbringing and the ability to finance such an education.

The cost of postsecondary education has increased exponentially in the past twenty to thirty years. As Emmie Martin, a reporter for CNBC, points out, college expenses are not directly be attributed to inflation. For the 1987-1988 academic year, a student at a private four-year college would have paid just $15,160. Today, that has increased to $34,740 (Martin, 2017). Therefore, the cost is now keeping many students from a higher education.

As you consider how knowledge is gained and applied throughout a lifetime, also consider how volunteer selection and training is impacted by its delivery. Gretchen Rubin points out in her book The Four Tendencies, how we acquire our understanding can impact how we deal with specific ideas. For example, she suggests grade-school students may question why they are learning about Mesopotamia because they do not get why the topic is important to them. In this case, thinking, analytical and searching skills are all necessary. As students age, skills such as these become more and more applicable. Learning about history and geography is fun for some, but there are also other factors at work.

While working on this book, I visited with individuals from different age groups. What has become clear to me is that Baby Boomers and older generations understand the importance of education and, in many cases, wish they would have had the opportunity to obtain more. Those who are younger learned from their parents and grandparents that education is important and that they could advance in their careers and in life. Additionally, more recent generations, Millennials for example, are realizing that just because they start out in one career does not mean that they will hold that position forever.

During an interview in the fall of 2017, I talked with a gentleman who was the residence hall director for a small private liberal-arts university. As we talked, I found myself sitting across from one of the most interesting and knowledgeable persons I have met in a long time. This man, a member of Generation X, stated that because of his educational and career background he finds himself identifying more with Generation Y. This individual, who I will call Alan, believed that his academics has been one of the biggest factors impacting his life and has been the driving force behind the jobs he has held and his transition into working as a residence hall director.

Formal Education

While post-secondary systems push four-year degrees, many are beginning to understand that the value of a two year, technical or trade certificate can be just as valuable in some fields. In addition, beginning an education in such a setting can establish the foundation to making the decision to obtain a four-year degree later in life.

While creating an internship program for high school students, I wanted to learn more about the value of trade and technical schools. I had the opportunity to talk with the wife of a long-time friend. All I knew about her was that she had worked as a hair stylist and had been a teacher at a cosmetology school. I received an attitude adjustment during our conversation. Up to that point, I had felt that everyone should complete high school and get, at a minimum, a bachelor's degree. During our discussion, I gained new appreciation for other types of training. She pointed out that it is possible for trades people to later use what they have learned in continuing their education. Specifically, she explained that cosmetology is more than learning to cut hair; it requires an understanding of chemistry and business. In her years of teaching, she knew of students who would later continue their education and expand their knowledge of these and other areas.

Informal Education

Informal learning from any situation is often misunderstood and under-represented. It can be embraced in many ways and, because of the expansion of technology, it has become even easier. Members of all generations are now familiar with the various ways to gain skills. In addition, it is now possible for individuals to expand skills by transitioning from one field of employment to another through informal learning, including self-study. Volunteers are able to use the same methods to gain new skills for their favorite nonprofit organization. Seniors wishing to volunteer based on their employment or educational history may choose to use self-study methods to ensure that they have the most current information.

When I was asked by my mother to design a website for her new business and to maintain all of her computer software, hardware and network elements; I immediately realized that while I had some ability, I needed to learn more. This began my exploration of technology, computer repair, and networking to upgrade my existing web design skills. Through this experience, I better recognized how individuals learn new skills. Over the years, many companies have begun offering courses and certification programs to employees at all levels. This keeps them current, engaged, learning new skills, and gives a return on their investment in terms of retention. The same concepts can be applied to volunteers. While the entire concept of this book focuses on past education and work experience, it is still important to remember that proficiencies need to be updated and that even volunteers who have had a thirty or forty-year career need to continue learning and sharpening skills.

Acquisition of new expertise is possible through companies such as linda.com and udemy.com. These sites provide a plethora of courses designed by qualified instructors on topics ranging from business management, consulting, design and technology. In the case of udemy.com, it is possible to create a customized curriculum. These offerings follow strict standards, and all courses must be approved by a team of moderators.

All these allow volunteers to pick up easily transferable skills. I became aware of a person with very little programming knowledge who took a course in IOS development and learned how to create applications for iPhone, iPad and Apple TV. When this happens, it demonstrates that people have the ability to learn, and it demonstrates to volunteer managers a willingness to expand.

As someone that engages in self-study daily, I believe it is important to find a method, or methods, that work best for you. As with most things, there is more than one way to learn. I like to read books on multiple subjects, then look for information on those topics from podcasts, academic journals and other sources. Sometimes the books I read come from doing the reverse of this action. Applying what you know can be done in a variety of ways and may not be applicable right away, but let what you are learning sink in and let you mind find ways to apply it.

Learning Styles

As I considered this chapter on educational background and learning styles, a quote often attributed to Buddha came to mind, "When the student is ready, the teacher will appear". This fits well for the discussion here. Regardless of the topic, it is important for individuals to recognize by which method they best learn; and from this, the teacher, or available source, will be made known.

Regardless of the format, there are sources available, so just understand how you best learn. Equally important is to know that it may be necessary to learn in different ways at different times.

Let us review the seven learning styles. Keep in mind that there is no right or wrong style for any one person and switching them is ok. The important factor here is to know your style. Discovering it can be a matter of experimentation and observation. If someone tells you that they believe learning in a different way may be helpful to you, give it a try!

- **Visual/Spatial:** Preference is given to using pictures, images, diagrams and spatial awareness.
- **Aural:** Preference is given to using sound and music.
- **Verbal:** Preference is given to using speech and words. Individuals who give prefer verbal learning often do so both orally and written.
- **Kinesthetic (Physical):** Preference to using their bodies and the sense of touch.
- **Logical:** Preference to utilizing logic, mathematics, reasoning and systems.
- **Social/Interpersonal:** Preference is given to learning in groups or with other people.
- **Solitary/Intrapersonal:** Preference is given to learning individually, often through self-study.

These are not just for internalizing information, but they can impact how you think, and how you choose words in both spoken and written communication. Science has demonstrated, through research conducted through imaging technology, that distinct parts of the brain are responsible for each learning style. Additionally, it is possible for you to change the way your brain works, allowing for new functions to take place.

The Brain

In "The Brain That Changes Itself: Stories of Personal Triumph from the Frontiers of Brain Science", Dr. Norman Doidge provides real-life examples of individuals who used meditation, brain training exercises and other techniques to create new neuropathways that effectively changed the way their brains work, process and retain information. In one instance, he gave an example of an individual who was paralyzed and was able to manipulate his own brain to make specific parts of this nonfunctioning body move.

Science is still working to understand how our complex bodies work, especially the brain. However, we know that it is divided into sectors that control speech, movement, thinking and emotion. Through technology, primarily mobile applications, is is now possible to work through puzzles and other activities to allow the brain to gain new skills or sharpen existing ones. While the technology is new, the concept of working the brain is not.

After conducting my own interviews and reading material developed by others, it has become apparent that engaging in certain exercises on a daily basis has emotional benefits. Doing the same with the brain is equally helpful. Using mobile applications such as Lumosity or even more traditional paper-based approaches such as crossword puzzles or word searches make the brain engage in new ways.

It is not possible to talk about older volunteers without addressing, at least to a degree, the degeneration of the brain through dementia and Alzheimer's disease. Work continues on understanding what causes these conditions. However, there are a few basic discoveries that can assist younger people in potentially avoiding these conditions in their later years, as well as help those currently struggling with them.

For many years, nursing homes in the United States have had "memory boxes" outside the rooms of patients struggling with cognition. These boxes contain articles that help in recognizing their rooms with things that are familiar to them. These are primarily from their long-term memory such as pictures of their children when they are younger or pictures of parents, pets and the like.

Engaging in mentally stimulating activities, proper diet and exercise combat cognitive decline. I have stated many times that daily activity such as crossword puzzles, walking, playing a musical instrument or engaging socially can be effective in prolonging memory. Throughout my research I have read a great deal about so called Blue Zones, areas of the world that contain more people who have lived to be at a minimum of one hundred years. One of the key elements of that zone is a diet containing high levels of plant consumption and less red meat. Another common aspect is that they commonly walk several miles per day either out of necessity, such as to transport water, or out of absolute desire to do it. Blue Zones are not the wealthiest part of the world, and in many instances they are sometimes the poorest. However, these folks are also some of the happiest. All of this sums up that older people who are mentally engaged also see little to no decline in mental ability.

Chapter 6
The Working World

When the idea of researching work experience came to my attention I will admit that I was intrigued, but at the same time hesitant. The intrigue came from my study of employee motivation during the writing of my master's thesis at Regis University. The hesitation was purely an uncertainty of how to narrow a topic and what exactly constituted "work experience." In the end, I am thankful that this element became part of my research, and it is now of great interest to me.

Both my parents worked, and, as a child, I had a pretty good idea of what they did and why. Everything they had done earlier in life progressively tied into what they did later. For example, my mother worked at the local Area Education Agency (AEA). I am certain that lead her to a secretarial position at a local group home, and after that she became a secretary for a government agency. That was eventually followed by her first selling real estate and then later selling insurance. She then moved to the nonprofit sector. The point here is that the various skills gained through each job gave her readiness necessary for her next career move.

While this seems just common sense, it is quite possible that we neglect the value of our past work experiences in our careers and life advancements. Considering previous skills can help us decide what type of assignment we may want to take next if we should stay in the position we are in, if we should return to school for additional education, or if we should retire early.

The experience workers gain varies from person to person, in part because they all have differing abilities in handling various levels of stress and applying their skills and education. As I studied work experiences, these two concepts stood out stronger than most: our motivation shifts from intrinsic to extrinsic as we age, as does the way people choose to apply themselves.

These elements are important, because, as people get older, they find themselves moving up the career ladder, or at least gaining additional responsibilities. The reason for career moves may be tied to six motives as originally defined by Dr. Lewis Terman (Shurkin, 1992). These motivations are defined as:

- **Values motives:** Acquiring new skills and knowledge.
- **Understanding motives:** Growing and developing
- **Enhancement motives:** Improving career prospects.
- **Career motives:** Aligning with expectations of their closest social circles
- **Social motives:** Offsetting negative feelings triggered by a sense of guilt, loneliness or other personal problems
- **Protective motives:** Protecting their own personal values.

Responses to these six motives will, in part, depend on people's work environment and generational affiliation. As being relatively young in my career, I may be more apt to react to the understanding motive because I value it and education. Someone nearing the end of their career may, in turn, respond more to the values motive.

Job vs. Career

At this point, I had to ask myself the obvious question, "What is a job?" After a look at the definition of "job" in the dictionary, I did what younger people (Generations Z and Alpha) may do and looked up the term on the internet. You guessed it, I found the definition on Wikipedia! "A job, or occupation is a person's role in society. More specifically, a job is an activity, often regular and performed in exchange for payment ("for a living.").

In many ways, it feels strange to be writing a section discussing the difference between a job and a career because, for me, there is an obvious, clear-cut distinction. However, the distinction between a life-long career versus holding many jobs is not being supported by our society and is not well defined in our educational system. It is further hindered by our culture that say that there are ways to "work less and make money" or to "get rich quick." These ideas have created a focus more on making money instead of building a long-lasting vocation or a strong set of skills that can be transferred between multiple careers, as may now be true among members of Generation Y, Z and most certainly within Generation Alpha.

While the United States Bureau of Labor Statistics says that the average person will hold ten jobs before the age of forty, this has not always been the case. I understand the necessity of changing jobs for numerous reasons, and as the ideals of younger generations evolve this may become even more of a necessity. However, I find it equally important for employees to feel comfortable staying in one place for a longer period of time as we have seen in older generations.

If we consider only the "role in society" part of this definition, we may arrive at some of the "get rich quick" elements mentioned earlier. This may also bring us to the current issues we find today, specifically the phenomenon of social media starts such as JoJo Siwa and others. According to Thrilllist.com, users spent over four million hours watching videos on YouTube and other media sites. In 2017, the number one video was of a person dancing while dressed as a giant oyster. While others point out that many of the most viral videos are inspiring and have assisted people in dealing with the stress of life, I find this trend to be disturbing at best.

The problem, in my opinion, is that the ability for someone to make a video and be lucky enough to have it go viral is giving our younger generation, specifically of generation Alpha and younger members of Generation Z, the wrong idea of what they want to do in terms of a career. This in turn could, and in my opinion most certainly will, have an impact on how members of these generations choose to engage as volunteers in both their younger and older years. Once again, I will point to my experience at AmeriCorps VISTA. Near the end of the 2018 school year, I was interviewing kindergarten through fifth grade students and asking them what careers they wanted. I was absolutely shocked when a few kids, boys mostly, told me that they wanted to be a "YouTuber." YouTuber is not a real word. (I could spin into another tangent about the younger generation making up words, but I will avoid that.) I was thankful that at least one of the boys who said that followed it up by saying, "If that doesn't work out I want to be a …".

While most people know that Millennials are changing jobs more than the older generations, and not necessarily in the same field. There is a stronger focus on transferable skills today. It is difficult for me to understand how people with no technology experience wind up working for a tech company. It happens because they have developed transferable skills and are able to readily learn new skills.

Structure and Career Level

While career structure and climbing the career ladder has not changed over the past several decades, the way employees reach various positions has changed a great deal. Those who have been working for the past forty to fifty years have experienced transitions within the same company and have had great success and received personal, professional and financial rewards.

The experience of the younger generations will be much different. The millennial generation has experienced career changes through education and training, and not through ascending the layers of an organization. By frequently transitioning between jobs, they have little to no longevity or employee benefits received by older generations.

My interviews in 2013 found that Baby Boomers, overall, were satisfied with their career choices and the field they chose. Their level of satisfaction appeared much higher than the those interviewed in 2018. From those college students in 2018 I learned that many of them had the desire to have great long careers, and one even understood the experiences of the Baby Boomers and wished to commit to one career.

Over the past four to six years, I have experienced a number of conversations and articles that point to the fact that our society should, and in some ways is, returning to the values held by prior generations.

Chapter 7
Crazy Happy

The term mental health is used by people to describe how they are feeling. For example, "I need to take a mental health day", or "I have mental health concerns about my grandmother." Additionally, one may say "I want to maintain positive mental health." The term implies that mental illness exists (Lysaght, Ouellette-Kuntz & Morrison, 2009; Ruddick, 2013). The bottom line is that most people are confused about what it really means because there is no good definition culturally or in the social sciences. Yes, dictionaries define it; for example, the Merriam-Webster dictionary defines it as:

The condition of being sound mentally and emotionally that is characterized by the absence of mental illness and by adequate adjustment especially as reflected in feeling comfortable about oneself, positive feelings about others, and the ability to meet the demands of daily life; also: the general condition of one's mental and emotional state.

The positive dimension of mental health is stressed in the World Health Organization's (WHO) constitution: "Health is a state of complete physical, mental and social well-being and not merely the absence of disease or infirmity." While this may come closest to a popular meaning, I feel that there is still room for clarification which will aid in gaining a deeper perception of how everyone can lead a happier, healthier life but will equally help in understanding those with thoughts or behaviors that, from a psychiatric or psychological standpoint, need attention.

As I began connecting education, work, and mental health, a basis for selecting volunteer positions developed, I needed a new definition of mental health for those who simply wish to live a better life, learn more, and grow both personally and for their communities—a definition of mental health for the every-day and sound-minded people that will allow individuals to learn and age together.

Some generalize it to mean social-wellbeing, or an individual's global happiness, which recognizes the ability of people to be generally happy with their situations and surroundings. Unlike mental health, social well-being demonstrates that an individual has some level of control over their destiny.

At this point, you could be wondering why I am arguing for a redefinition of mental health at all when there is a strong definition of social well-being. The answer to this question is simple. The term social well-being, at least in my opinion, is one that most people will not use. Someone is not going to say "I do not feel good, I need social well-being day." The term itself is overly complex and still leaves room for misunderstanding. It does not fully embrace individuals, but rather society as a whole.

The new definition for mental health for the social sciences will assist individuals in aligning future research, practices, and beliefs for the good of humanity. Therefore, mental health for purposes of volunteer management and other social science disciplines shall be defined as: "An individual's overall satisfaction with life goals and objectives as they relate to daily social, cultural and economic activities."

This definition allows individuals to focus on their own goals and objectives, change them when necessary, and adapt to changing personal, economic, community and technological circumstances. Variations within these elements will allow the individual to grow personally, and as a part of a larger community.

In order to maintain positive mental health, it is necessary to engage in mentally and physically stimulating activities, including exercise, involvement with community organizations and volunteering. Overall, mental health may be partly dependent on the quality of life and social well-being of individuals, which is experienced by each person differently. Therefore, it is vital for us to understand our needs and desires during the retirement years.

Family and Values

Growing up in rural Iowa gave me a clear-cut sense of right and wrong, strong values related to work, and how I should interact with others. My core values may not be easily understood by someone who is not from my state or the region. The basic idea that one gains ethics through family ties is commonly held; however, standards can also be acquired through social and cultural connections and can change over time. The way they are developed, held and changed evolves and, in some cases, may even be revert to those held by previous generations.

Child development experts tell us that children around two years old will commonly begin helping with, or mimicking through play, various household chores including cleaning and cooking. They also begin role-playing careers, so while stereotypical roles are beginning to disappear for children, in their play they are still present.

As younger people, such as generation Y--and even generation Z, begin having children, the values being taught are changing. For example, I know a young couple who, prior to the birth of their baby girl, decided not to find out her gender, but instead furnish her room with gender-neutral furniture and clothe her in non-specific clothing. Their hope was that she would have the ability to make her own gender choices and have a more open view of the world and what she would be able to do in life.

I do not ever recall a time, at least as a child, when I was not happy. Sure, there were times that I was mad, upset or angry about something, but I was never truly unhappy. This, at least partially, I believe resulted from the values of my family and the experiences and tools I was exposed to. Even growing up legally blind as a result of hydrocephalus, I was not down or depressed. Sure, I didn't like being in the hospital, going through countless MRI and CAT scans, and even going through shuntogram and shunt tap procedures. If anything, those experiences made me stronger and gave me the desire to help others who had similar difficulties.

Being legally blind in the 1980s also meant that I had to work extra hard to access my education. Besides the necessary advocacy work, most of it came through technology. As we will learn when we talk about generation Alpha, some parents today are choosing to limit, or completely stop their children's availability to electronics. However, my experience was quite the opposite. There was a continuous search for the right technology to meet my needs and a constant personal desire to know more about computers. Today science is telling us that too much "screen time" is a bad thing. While I can understand this, and agree to some extent, it can also lead to a great deal of learning and to developing critical thinking skills.

I firmly believe that it was the commitment of my parents and my extended family to life-long learning that gave me the desire and the support to continuously learn through and about technology. A supportive family environment for anyone who wants to gain knowledge can be a great thing. For example, in families who value music, the same processes take place.

Stay Mentally Strong

Staying mentally strong may be one of the biggest factors to longevity. When asked what keeps them "young", many older Americans point to things such as volunteering, friendships, and continued engagement in the community or pursuit of knowledge. During my initial study in 2014, a volunteer pointed out that doing crossword puzzles was the biggest thing that kept her mentally sharp. She had developed her mother's habit and intends to continue with it for as long as possible.

Abraham Maslow pointed out that social engagement is an essential part of our nature. While it is possible for some to live in isolation, it is not common and can cause some to go crazy or have many social and/or psychological defects. There are people who will bring about immediate visions of isolation, lack of social inclusion and even mental instability. One of them is Ted Kaczynski, more commonly known as the Unabomber, who wreaked havoc on the United States through mail bombs. Between 1978 and 1995, he mailed sixteen bombs across the United States. It has been found that reclusive individuals often have a disdain for our society, the government or other social reasons for living outside of the norm. While Maslow would have been aware of them, knowledge has increased over the past several decades.

While the above may seem scary and strange, it is equally important to note that at times people choose to live in isolation for deeply personal, and even professional reasons. For example, Henry David Thoreau lived for a time next to Walden Pond. He reflected on his experience in a book by the same name. Over the past two or three years, I have seen many signs that our culture may be encouraging this type of escape from society. Organizations such as the Windcall Institute encourage organizational professionals to take three weeks to get away from everything to reflect and revitalize.

Being mentally able may be partly dependent on individual needs. However, cultural elements exist that support mental happiness. Dan Butner, founder of the Blue Zones concept, points out nearly thirty percent of Danish residents volunteer. Is it possible that engagement is what makes them some of the happiest in the world? However, according to the Corporation for National and Community Service (CNCS), the United States is only about five percent lower (around 25.3%) than Denmark. Yet the United States ranks eighteenth according to the 2018 happiness report released by the Sustainable Development Solutions Network. So, what is different?

Maximize Your Skills

In his original hierarchy of needs, Abraham Maslow demonstrated the concept of self-actualization, where people reach their highest potential. That will vary from person to person. For example, one may reach it by earning a bachelor's degree while another from a similar socioeconomic background may only reach it by earning a terminal degree. How skills are developed depends on the individual. However, factors exist that will influence peoples' decisions and their ability to maximize their skills.

As I am sure you have heard that the people you surround yourself with are the people you will become like. Therefore, if you choose to associate with highly motivated people, you yourself will most likely become highly motivated. The inverse is also true. If you surround yourself with unmotivated people who engage in lazy behavior such as constant game-playing, watching television or not working, this will most likely be reflected in your behavior. However, there are rare occasions that these are not the cases.

Habits and Attitudes

Sometime around late 2016, I opened my e-mail to the latest issue of the Help A Reporter Out (HARO) query. It is a great way for writers, reporters and the like to finding people to help with their communication projects. On that particular day, I learned of an author who was looking for those who would write about their daily habits and attitudes. For some odd reason, I decided to submit an entry. Several months later I received a notice that I had been selected as one of fifty-two individuals to be part of a new book, Habits and Attitudes, being compiled by Dr. Lance A. Cazza. Over his life and career as a chiropractor he had discovered how important strong habits and attitudes are. The writers in his book were to give their ideas, as well as a "parting shot" where they give one final piece of advice.

Obviously strong habits have been a part of my entire life, or I don't think I would have made it into his book. Habits can change but having certain things that you do every day is important for your mental and emotional health. Writing my contribution to the book made me reflect on my original dissertation and helped me fully make the connection between habits and attitudes and volunteers.

For many older people, it is easier to identify good habits that they do every day, or nearly every day. Their general attitudes of life are usually cemented by the time they reach retirement. However, this may also apply to younger generations as well, depending on their upbringing. For me, making my bed, calling my grandparents and volunteering was a habit. Some I did every day and some every week. Not to divulge my entire section in Dr. Cazza's book, but a few of my daily habits include: making family a priority, getting up and getting going, and making social media less of a priority. My attitudes mostly come from a strong positive outlook. For the rest of my thoughts, you will have to read Dr. Cazza's book!

To sit and think about your habits and attitudes, you may arrive at some interesting conclusions. In my opinion, it is a chicken or an egg question. Dr. Cazza points out that habits come before attitudes, but I personally think it could go either way, and neither way is the right way. In my humble opinion, attitudes may change informal habits, but, as I think over my life, the attitudes of others may have influenced my habits which then formed my attitudes. The direction this flows may partly depend on culture and/or family.

In the world of volunteering, I believe that strong habits and attitudes can greatly affect the overall mental health of a volunteer. If there are daily tasks or rituals that help them maintain their sense of self, the organization should be able to find ways to build these into the position description, or at last have an understanding of their habits and attitudes. This can be gained through the interview process or through daily interaction and the continued training of the volunteer.

Chapter 8
Have You Ever Thought about Conducting Your Own Research?

This chapter is written out of my experience to those who may want to add new insights with their own studies. The desire to help people is one of the primary reasons I decided to continue my education after obtaining my undergraduate degree. At the time, it was my understanding that a Master's degree would give me the tools to do everything I wanted to in terms of a career. However, I quickly determined that the degree was simply a way to acquiring more knowledge and learning additional research skills. It was not useful in ways I wanted, as most would not consider what I would write because I did not have the terminal degree making me an "expert" in my field. With a Master's I was able to help people, and I learned how to start organizations and evaluate programs, but that was all.

While becoming an "expert" at Capella University, the true lesson I experienced was that I did not know everything, and I never would know it all; but that people would nevertheless look to me. I also discovered that once my research was complete, it was important to identify what was still missing and what someone else could do in the future.

The traditional format for a doctoral dissertation is to include suggestions for additional research. Dissertations can be dry, so it is rare for someone outside of academia to read them. However, I find it strange that more mainstream publications do not contain the challenge of future research possibilities. By doing so, more individuals may be encouraged to continue their education, ask questions and incorporate their own research into popular culture. I am not saying that there is not a place for terminal degree holders, there is and always will be; but what I am saying is that the everyday person can develop and incorporate their own ideas into their organizations and communities. This will allow our society to advance.

As with any sound scientific study, one of the best ways to insure valid research is to ensure that the methods to design and collect the data are clearly outlined and can be easily duplicated by another researcher. Therefore, it is necessary for the original study to be so well written that anyone can replicate it. I welcome you to review the research in this book, understand it, develop it, compare your findings, and let the world know what you found.

Upon the completion of any study, it is important to review what was learned, and, in this case, what was not. Realizing what you do not know is the only way to identify areas of future needs. In the case of volunteerism in rural communities, one of the first issues I identified was that there was no distinction between formal and informal education. In my initial writing I identified that formal education would be the basis for the topic of education; however, I understood that there is value to informal education. I am by no means advocating that there is no place for formal education. But I understand that for some generations the attaining an education past a certain point simply was not possible, and these individuals learned how to acquire knowledge in other ways and to apply this expertise for personal and professional advancement.

Separate studies showed volunteers indeed gain helpful enlightenment from both informal and formal education, and both are vital in considering the selection of those to fill voluntary positions. If you would feel the need to do such a study, you may wish to remove the work and/or mental health components from your study. In that case, a change in only one factor would be shown to be vital.

There is potential for virtual volunteerism research. However, it is sometimes difficult to talk about technology and seniors in the same sentence. Although technology is not uncommonly used by today's seniors, it is not as common as it is with generations X or Y or the Net Generation. It is important to realize that technological access is sometimes difficult for rural Iowans, and not just the senior cohort. However, an exploration of virtual possibilities within a rural senior population would bring increased awareness, discover more opportunities, and uncover additional skill resources.

For example, an Iowa nurse could volunteer to write the health content for awareness organizations, author nursing publications for community groups, or provide remote answering services to crisis victims. Virtual engagement is an area with nearly endless opportunities. Since little research has been done in this area, a connection between virtual volunteerism and rural communities would be of great benefit to them.

I had a certain degree of difficulty when determining formal and informal education acquisition and volunteer application in my study. As a result, I made no distinction. During my interview process, every individual was a "traditional volunteer", even though some did not graduate high school while a few achieved a post-secondary degree. However, the potential exists for research regarding formal verses informal education and how each impacts the selection of volunteers for positions. This type of research would keep the work experience component the same.

Additionally, formal and informal volunteer settings must be explored. As a rule, informal volunteerism is difficult to track because individuals do things for family and friends. For example, an individual who cares for grandchildren on a regular basis with no pay and gives of their resources is, in a sense, volunteering.

Validating a study is possibly one of the most important factors surrounding research. While using only one research method makes completion of the study much simpler, increased validity can be brought through multiple methods. Future study of rural volunteerism could be done through additional interviews. However, adding a questionnaire would make it easier to obtain more data in a shorter period of time. For example, a set of interviews could be conducted as I did, but the questionnaire could be given to another sample group in an effort to obtain more data.

While information collecting methods are different, questions on the questionnaire can use common themes from interviews. For example, a questionnaire may ask "Do you believe your past work experience influenced the selection of your current volunteer role?" An individual would select "yes" or "no." An individual may then be asked "If yes, why" then select from a list of common themes such as "I use skills from my career", "I utilize technology used in my career" and "I volunteer to make use of my professional skills."

Aside from duplicating this study and gaining additional perspectives from volunteers; if the identified areas (past work experiences, educational background and additional development of the new definition of mental health) were to be explored, they could greatly increase our understanding of how these three elements can play a role in the selection and retention of volunteers.

As my ideas evolved and I began writing this book, I discovered happiness as a new area of research. There are no scientific studies regarding this; however, a small amount of popular literature and media presentations are being created surrounding this topic. The exploration of happiness and the interaction it may have, in part or as a whole in the selection of and impact on volunteers and their mental health, is vital. Although it may be assumed that happiness automatically connects to day-to-day mental health, no formal study has yet to been conducted to explore this concept.

Available resources provide outlines of various generational characteristics, however, they are not adequate enough to contribute information for each type of study. Therefore, as has been done in this text, those wishing to expand on the subjects at hand should consider conducting their own generational search and analysis.

As noted in the preface, the exploration of senior volunteers came from a desire to craft a well-rounded dissertation in a timely manner and avoid a great deal of problems with the Institutional Review Board. As a result, my original idea of a study of youth was discarded. However, I suggest a study in motivational factors of youth in the selection of voluntary opportunities. This type of study would provide nonprofit and community organizations with greater details, allowing for more appropriate marketing efforts in recruiting young people.

Expansion of the concepts of education, work, and mental health across the generations would not only provide for increased data on generational values, but would also allow for the development of a model of volunteerism based on the established factors. Studies targeted at the six living generations regarding education, work (or attitudes toward work), and mental health will add another layer of expansion of these new ideas in voluntary service.

As noted in the Terman Study, gathering information over several generations is helpful for a multifaceted approach by collecting data from numerous sources. While it is understood that such a study would be time consuming and costly, it could quite possibly be one of the best ways to confirm the concepts proposed in this text. Addressing such a study with questions similar to those in the Appendix, along with an expansion on demographic data and insights from individuals close to the participant, would be ideal.

A great deal of the formal study on the topic of volunteerism has been conducted in the United Kingdom, Canada and a small portion in the United States. While research has also been conducted in China and other countries in that region, the relevance of such literature could not be initially found because of the vast cultural differences. Through the expansion of technology, ease of travel and the sharing of cultures, it may be possible to blend such research with the fore-mentioned countries. If such merging were to take place, it would be necessary to note important cultural and personal differences of the participants.

My hope is that as you have been reading, you have been thinking about the future, have been asking yourself questions and hopefully writing these questions down. I welcome you to take my ideas and twist them, manipulate them and make them your own. I also hope that our paths cross so we can discuss your own ideas coupled with mine to see what new information and ideas can be created.

Appendix A
Traditional Volunteer Application

Note: This application can be downloaded at jessebolinger.com

For decades, nonprofit agencies have used traditional application forms to collect information about people. Each organization has its own adoption of this questionnaire, and reviewing it will help you understand how existing ones can be modified, how new ones can be created to best utilize volunteers' past experiences, and how these changes can assist in maintaining their positive mental health.

Volunteer Application

First Name _____
Last Name _____
Address _____
City/State/Zip _____
Telephone (_____)_____-_____
E-mail _____
Date of Birth _____
Spouse's Name _____
Physical Limitations: ___ No ___ Yes
(If yes, please explain) _____

Education _____

Former work/occupation _____
Most recent employer (optional) _____
List previous volunteer experience below
Organization Name: _____
Dates of service: _____
Contact Person: _____
Phone Number: _____
E-mail Address: _____

Please describe your activities:

_____

Organization Name: _____
Dates of service: _____
Contact Person: _____
Phone Number: _____
E-mail Address: _____
Please describe your activities:

_____
_____

Organization Name: _____
Dates of service: _____
Contact Person: _____
Phone Number: _____
E-mail Address: _____
Please describe your activities:

Skills (List any skills you feel may be helpful)

_____
_____
_____

Volunteer availability: (Circle all applicable)
Number of Days per week: 1 2 3 4 5
Number of hours per week:_____
Monday Tuesday Wednesday Thursday Friday Virtual No Preference
What type of volunteer work are you most interested in?
____ Fundraising ___ Letter Writing ___ Database creation/update
___ Presentations ___ Technology ___ Other_____
In an emergency, notify:
First Name _____
Last Name _____

Calling All Volunteers 99

Address _____
City/State/Zip _____
Telephone_____
Is this volunteer experience being conducted as an internship?
_____ Yes _____ No

(If you wish to conduct your volunteer work to satisfy requirements for an academic internship, please attach internship guidelines and contact information for your academic advisor or internship coordinator.)

I certify that all information provided in this application and attached documents is accurate and correct to the best of my knowledge.

_____
(Signature/Volunteer)   (Date)

_____
(Signature/Staff)   (Date)

Appendix B
The New Way

Note: This application can be downloaded at jessebolinger.com

Throughout this book, you have learned how volunteers' educational background, past work experience and mental health can be utilized in the selection of volunteer positions. With this in mind, it is necessary to modify the application form, the interview and the retention processes. As an interviewer, apply this sample pattern to aid in modifying your own questionnaire, or, as an applicant, think about how you will complete forms with organizations that use a traditional format.

Volunteer Application
    First Name _____
    Last Name _____
    Address _____
    City/State/Zip _____
    Telephone(____)_____-_____
    E-mail_____
    Date of Birth _____
    Spouse's Name _____
    Physical Limitations: ___ No___ Yes
    (Please explain any limitations)_____
_____

Please fill out all applicable information. If you wish to provide any additional information, please do so at the bottom of this form.
    Education: (Continue up to your highest level.)
    School name: _____
    City/State: _____
    Grade/years completed:_____
    Area of Study _____
    Degree/certificate received: _____

School name: _____
City/State: _____
Grade/years completed: _____
Area of Study _____
Degree/certificate received: _____
School name: _____
City/State: _____
Grade/years completed: _____
Area of Study _____
Degree/certificate received: _____
School name: _____
City/State: _____
Grade/years completed: _____
Area of Study _____
Degree/certificate received: _____

Please describe any informal education you have obtained (i.e. non-credit online courses, community education programs etc.)

_____
_____
_____
_____
_____
_____

Work Experience:

What type of work would you consider yourself having the highest skill level in? ____Accounting ___ Administrative Support ___ Aerospace ___ Banking___ Business Administration ___ Computer Science/Information Technology ____ Construction ____ Engineering ____ Home-maker ____ Other _____

Most recent Employer: _____
Length of employment: _____
Reason for leaving: _____
Please describe your work: _____
_____
_____

Calling All Volunteers

Employer: _____
Length of employment: _____
Reason for leaving: _____

Please describe your work: _____
_____
_____

Employer: _____
Length of employment: _____
Reason for leaving: _____

Please describe your work: _____
_____
_____

Employer: _____
Length of employment: _____
Reason for leaving: _____

Please describe your work: _____
_____
_____

Employer: _____
Length of employment: _____
Reason for leaving: _____

Please describe your work: _____
_____
_____

List previous volunteer experience: _____
_____
_____

_____
_____
_____

_____
    Skills (List any skills you feel may be helpful) _____
_____
_____

Everyday Life

    What kind of things make you happy?

_____
_____
_____

_____
    Do specific daily activities help you maintain who you are?
    ___Yes ___No
    If so, what are these activities? _____
_____
_____
_____
_____

Volunteer availability: (Circle all applicable)

    Number of Days per week: 1 2 3 4 5
    Number of hours per week:_____
    Monday   Tuesday   Wednesday   Thursday   Friday
    Virtual   No Preference
    What type of volunteer work are you most interested in?
    ____Fundraising____ Letter Writing____ Database creation/update
    ____Presentations____ Technology____ Other_____

Emergency Contact

    First Name_____
    Last Name_____
    Address _____

City/State/Zip_____
Telephone_____
Is this volunteer experience being conducted as an internship?
___ Yes___ No
(If you wish to conduct your volunteer work to satisfy requirements for an academic internship, please attach internship guidelines and contact information for your academic advisor or internship coordinator.)

Is there any other information you would like to share?
_____
_____
_____
_____
_____

I certify that all information provided in this application and attached documents is accurate and correct to the best of my knowledge.

(Signature/Volunteer) _____
(Date) _____
(Signature/Staff) _____
(Date) _____

Appendix C
Interview Questions

To Those Doing Research:

Assisting others interested in conducting research in the area of volunteerism has been important to me. As a result, I want to share some of the tools I used during my research. Please consider these questions as you review my work and envision how you may be able to expand on it through formal academic study or through less formal work within your organization or community.

Also included here is a list of demographic questions I took advantage of at various points in my research. Developing your own demographic questions is important to your exploration of any topic. Create questions based on your own needs and never use them to discriminate, but only use the responses to draw comparisons or demonstrate differences in populations.

As always, the protection of personal information is important. To do this, please insure that you obtain the proper clearance through organizational staff, university officials or any other review processes that may be in place. While you may desire to conduct specific research for your own personal educational advancement, obtaining this approval is still necessary and vital to protect those involved in your study.

To Everyone: Learn More and Share Your Thoughts

I want this book, and the ideas within, to be an ongoing process and conversation for you. Please feel free to visit my website to learn more about current research, and/or subscribe to my blog and share your input. **www.jessebolinger.com**

Interview Questions for Children

1. What do you want to be when you grow up?
2. Why do you want to be that?
3. Do you like to help others?
4. Why do you like to help other people?
5. Do you want to help others when you are older?
6. What makes you happy?
7. Do you have something you do every day that makes you happy? What is it?
8. Do you like a small town or a big city better?
9. Why do you like or dislike living in a small town.
10. What do you think about older people?
11. What does it mean to be old?
12. Can older people do the same things as younger people?
13. Can older people help others?
14. Do you want to tell me anything else?

Interview Questions for Young Adults/College Students

1. After completing your education, what type of work would you like to do?
2. Do you have a job of some kind?
3. How has living in a rural area impacted your ability to utilize past experiences, either related to work or education, in volunteer position selection?
4. Have you been involved in volunteer activities through your school? If so, what kind of activities. If not, why have you not been involved.
5. Can you please tell me how you may utilize your past education, any work experience you have and future education and work experience you may get to select volunteer positions when you are older?
6. If you have held a job, did your employer encourage you to volunteer? If so, how?
7. How do you view mental health? What do you do to remain mentally alert?
8. What makes you happy?
9. How has living in a rural environment impacted your mental health?
10. Why do you like or dislike living in a rural area?
11. How do you think your mental health will impact your future selection of volunteer positions based on your education and work experience?
12. Do you have any final thoughts you would like to add at this time?

Interview Questions for Working Adults

1. What type of work do you do presently and what other jobs have you held?
2. Do you volunteer anywhere? If so, where?
3. If you do not volunteer, can you explain why not?
4. How has living in a rural area impacted your ability to utilize past experiences, either related to work or education, in volunteer position selection?
5. What is your highest level of education and why is this the highest level you achieved?
6. Were you involved in volunteer activities during formal education? If so, what types of activities were you involved in? If you were not involved in volunteer activities why not?
7. Can you please state your personal beliefs regarding how past work experience and educational background impact the selection of volunteer positions?
8. Has your current employer, or any past employer, encourage volunteer activity? If so how did your employer encourage this involvement?
9. How do you view mental health? What do you do to remain mentally alert?
10. How has living in a rural environment impacted your mental health?
11. How has your mental health impacted the selection of a volunteer position based on your education and work experience?
12. Do you have any final thoughts you would like to add at this time?

Interview Questions for Retired Individuals

1. Prior to retirement, what type of work did you do? What other types of jobs have you held?
2. How has living in a rural area impacted your ability to utilize past experiences, either related to work or education, in volunteer position selection?
3. What is your highest level of education and why is this the highest level you achieved?
4. Were you involved in volunteer activities during formal education? If so, what types of activities were you involved in? If you were not involved in volunteer activities why not?
5. Can you please state your personal beliefs regarding how past work experience and educational background impact the selection of volunteer positions?
6. Did your employer encourage volunteer activity? If so how did your employer encourage this involvement?
7. How do you view mental health? What do you do to remain mentally alert?
8. How has living in a rural environment impacted your mental health?
9. How has your mental health impacted the selection of a volunteer position based on your education and work experience?
10. Do you have any final thoughts you would like to add at this time?

Demographic Questions

Participant name_____
Date_____
Gender____Male ____Female
Age_____   Year born_____   Generation identified with_____
Race_____
Grade in school (If not applicable write N/A)_____
Year retired (If not applicable write N/A)_____
Community_____
Was this information obtained from a parent____Yes____No

Works Cited

Adams, R., (2016). Secondary schools face sharpest cuts to funding since 1970s, says thinktank. *The Guardian*, Friday 15th April. Available from http://www.theguardian.com/education/2016/apr/15/secondary-schools-sharpest-cuts-funding-since-1970s-thinktank[Accessed 20th March 2019].

Ajzen, I. (1985). From intentions to actions: A theory of planned behavior. In J. Kuhl & J. Beckman (Eds.), *Action-control: From cognition to behavior* (pp. 11- 39). Heidelberg, Germany: Springer.

Ajzen, I. (1991). The theory of planned behavior. *Organizational Behavior and Human Decision Processes*, 50, 179-211.

Ajzen, I. (2006). Constructing a TPB questionnaire: Conceptual and methodologicalconsiderations. Originally prepared by September, 2002; Revised January, 2006. Retrieved from http://people.umass.edu/aizen/pdf/tpb.measurement.pdf

Apple Inc. (2016, June 13). Keynote - WWDC 2016 - Videos. Retrieved August 03, 2018, from https://developer.apple.com/videos/play/wwdc2016/101/

Bolinger, J. O. (2010). *Employee Performance and Motivation: Study and Application for Graceland University* (Unpublished master's thesis). Regis University.

Bush, G. W. (2002, January 29). President Delivers State of the Union Address. Retrieved October 21, 2018, from https://georgewbush-whitehouse.archives.gov/news/releases/2002/01/20020129-11.html

Chapman, G. D., & White, P. E. (2012). *The 5 languages of appreciation in the workplace: Empowering organizations by encouraging people.* Chicago: Northfield Pub.

Corporation for National and Community Service. (n.d.). Statutes, Regulations, and Policies. Retrieved December 1, 2018, from https://www.nationalservice.gov/about/open-government-initiative/policies-and-procedures

Corporation for National and Community Service. (2018). National timeline: Corporation for national and community service. Retrieved from http://www.nationalservice.gov/about/who-we-are/out-history/national-service-timeline

Hartman, S. (2018, May 04). 4-year-old superhero using his power to feed the homeless. Retrieved November 21, 2018, from https://www.cbsnews.com/news/austin-perine-alabama-4-year-old-superhero-using-his-power-to-feed-the-homeless/

Huffington, A. S. (2017). *The sleep revolution: Transforming your life, one night at a time.* New York: Harmony Books.

Jorgenson, J., & Schneider, C. G. (2017). *Open air: How people like yourself are changing the aviation industry.* Franklin, TN: Traitmarker Books.

Kelly Services Inc., (2009). How to maintain employee motivation. Retrieved March 28, 2009, from How to Maintain Employee Motivation Web site: http://www.kellyit.com/eprise/main/web/us/hr_manager/articles_jan08_Maintain_Employee_Motivation?

Kenrick, D.T., Griskevicius, V., Neuberg, S.L., & Schaller, M. (2010). Renovating the pyramid of needs: Contemporary extensions built upon ancient foundations. *Perspectives on Psychological Science*, 5, 292–314.

Lysaght, R., Ouellette-Kuntz, H., & Morrison, C. (2009). Meaning and value of productivity to adults with intellectual disabilities. *Intellectual and Developmental Disabilities*, 47(6), 413-424.

Marcus, D. L. (2000, February 21). Generation X turns out to be generous. U.S. News & World Report, 128(7), 54. Retrieved from http://link.galegroup.com/apps/doc/A59458368/AONE?u=ialamoni&sid=AONE&xid=58e62b54

Martin, E. (2017, November 29). Here's how much more expensive it is for you to go to college than it was for your parents. Retrieved December 17, 2018, from https://www.cnbc.com/2017/11/29/how-much-college-tuition-has-increased-from-1988-to-2018.html

Maslow, A. H. (1943). A theory of human motivation. *Psychological Review*, 50(4), 370-396. doi:10.1037/h0054346

Maslow, A. H. (1969). The farther reaches of human nature. *Journal of Transpersonal Psychology*, 1(1), 1–9.

Royal College of Nursing, (12 November 2008). Small rewards and expressions of thanks improve motivation. *Nursing Standard*. 23.10.

Shurkin, J. N. (1992). *Terman's kids: The groundbreaking study of how the gifted grow up*. Little, Brown and Co.

Volunteer Success Stories. (n.d.). Retrieved from http://www.pqchc.com/volunteers-students/volunteer-success-stories

CPSIA information can be obtained
at www.ICGtesting.com
Printed in the USA
FFHW010009050919
54721761-60433FF